# TABLES &
# PLATFORMS

# TABLES & PLATFORMS

*FORGING IDENTITY AND CHARACTER
FOR A LIFE OF INFLUENCE*

## MARIOS ELLINAS

SON OF THUNDER PUBLICATIONS

Published by Son of Thunder Publications, sonofthunderpublications.org

Cover design by Gabrial Heath
Interior design based on a book layout ©2017 by BookDesignTemplates.com, with additional elements by Rachel L. Hall
Edited by Rachel L. Hall

Scripture quotations marked (AMP) are taken from the Amplified Bible, Copyright © 1954, 1958, 1962, 1964, 1965, 1987 by The Lockman Foundation. Used by permission.

Scripture quotations marked (ESV) are from The ESV® Bible (The Holy Bible, English Standard Version®), copyright © 2001 by Crossway, a publishing ministry of Good News Publishers. Used by permission. All rights reserved."

Scripture marked EXB is taken from The Expanded Bible. Copyright ©2011 by Thomas Nelson. Used by permission. All rights reserved.

Scriptures marked KJ2000 are taken from the King James 2000 version. Copyright © 2000, 2003, 2001. Dr. Robert A. Couric. Used by permission.

Scripture quotations marked (NIV) are taken from the Holy Bible, New International Version®, NIV®. Copyright © 1973, 1978, 1984, 2011 by Biblica, Inc.™ Used by permission of Zondervan. All rights reserved worldwide. www.zondervan.com The "NIV" and "New International Version" are trademarks registered in the United States Patent and Trademark Office by Biblica, Inc.™

Scriptures marked NKJV are taken from the from the NEW KING JAMES VERSION®. Copyright© 1982 by Thomas Nelson, Inc. Used by permission. All rights reserved.

Scripture marked (TLV) is taken from the Holy Scriptures, Tree of Life Version. Copyright © 2014,2016 by the Tree of Life Bible Society. Used by permission of the Tree of Life Bible Society.

Scripture quotations marked (TPT) are from The Passion Translation®. Copyright © 2017, 2018 by Passion & Fire Ministries, Inc. Used by permission. All rights reserved. ThePassionTranslation.com.

Published in the United Kingdom for worldwide distribution.

Tables and Platforms: Forging Identity and Character for a Life of Influence/ Marios Ellinas. —1st ed.

ISBN 978-1-7321638-7-4 Paperback
ISBN 978-1-1911251-45-3 eBook

# Acknowledgments

My heartfelt thanks to Heather Rayner and her team for all the hard work towards this publication, to Rachel Hall for her professional editing expertise and excellent service, to Gabrial Heath for the cover design, to the Revelation Partners team for transcriptions of my talks, to Ian Clayton for being a great friend and mentor, to Danielle, Christos, Caleb, and Chloe—the best family I could have hoped for, to the leaders and congregation of Valley Shore for their constant support, and to my parents for their unconditional love and for always having my back.

*Marios Ellinas*
*Connecticut, USA*
*September 2019*

# Contents

# Introduction

*...No book or training course can adequately prepare you for a moment like that. You don't have time to evaluate the proposal... You must respond immediately—and what you say can change things...*

IT WAS A BEAUTIFUL DAY in one of my favorite places in the world. After a week of assignments there, I was scheduled to fly out late that evening. A good friend had arranged a meeting at a small restaurant in one of the city's malls. We rode together for about an hour, catching up on the happenings in our lives, before settling into one of the restaurant's booths for lunch.

The purpose of the luncheon was to introduce me to a businessman my friend had known since college. My friend spoke highly of this young entrepreneur and was excited the meeting was finally happening.

The man arrived promptly at the appointed time. He was everything I had been led to expect and more. He was charismatic, brilliant, engaging, genuine. His eyes reflected depth and strength of character, and his body language showed high self-esteem, tempered with humility.

Just minutes after initial niceties and ordering our meals, we engaged in deep, meaningful conversation. We talked for a long time and ate well. Every time we shared our viewpoints and explained our understanding about a topic, it felt as though waves of revelation were washing over us. I cannot recall what subjects we covered, but I vividly remember the sentiment—we were all amply edified and encouraged by our interaction. The luncheon was absolutely refreshing.

When it came time to part, the young entrepreneur and I exchanged numbers and promised to stay in touch. Then, with his hand extended towards me, he said, "I'd like to recommend you to come and speak for us."

I looked at his outstretched arm, and time seemed to freeze.

The "us" he wanted me to speak to wasn't referring to a future lunch gathering among friends; nor was it a speaking engagement within the man's business community. I knew from prior conversations that "us" was a massive, exceptionally impactful church in that nation. It was a church with global influence led by one of the most charismatic leaders in the world.

I never saw it coming—the implied invitation caught me completely off guard. What to do? What to say?

Imagine yourself in that position. No book or training course can adequately prepare you for a moment like that. You don't have time to evaluate the proposal. Your phone's been off since the meeting started—you have no means of quickly contacting and consulting your spouse. There is no chance to seek counsel from mentors or close confidants. Even taking the time to silently pray a quick prayer could negatively affect the momentum.

The man's extended hand waits to shake yours. He has already made up his mind about you—you're in. He's made his offer and expects your answer. You must respond immediately —speaking out of the abundance of your heart—and what you say can change things, significantly.

For many people employed in my line of work, the invitation "Speak for us" would appear a dream come true assignment. But it wasn't for me, and it never will be. Because of a decision I made a long time ago, without even blinking—my eyes locked on his, a broad smile on my face—I gently bumped the back of his hand with mine and said, "I wouldn't be interested in that right now. I would prefer to grow in relationship with you."

---

Tables and platforms are the two main venues through which we can influence and serve the people around us. A lunch meeting arranged by a mutual friend facilitated my acquaintance with the young entrepreneur: thus, our relationship started at a table. What transpired at the restaurant prompted my new friend to suggest a platform event at which I would be the speaker.

As physical objects, tables and platforms resemble one another: they are frequently rectangular in shape and both have raised, flat surfaces. Yet the purpose of each is unique. One places those gathered around it on the same level, allowing relationships to develop through conversation and an interchange of ideas. The other raises one person higher than the rest of those gathered, allowing that person's message to be communicated to the crowd.

For the purposes of this publication, I present *tables* as small-group settings for conversation where relationships develop. On the other hand, *platforms* represent those venues where our efforts have broader influence and impact. The two are connected. Most of my platform assignments—whether speaking engagements, publications, or large-group consultations—originated at a table. By the same token, any successful platform task has inevitably led to more table interactions.

In most cases, the terms *table* and *platform* are not literal. A table meeting may look like a personal phone call, a car ride through traffic, or a group of friends conversing while strolling on a beach. A platform may be a YouTube channel, an art exhibit, a TV show on which one may be a host or guest, a teacher's classroom or even a book like this one.

I was fascinated with platforms for many years. I closely observed those who stood on various platforms of influence, and I aspired to be just like them. I dreamed about glorious moments when I would be introduced to large audiences, and I daydreamed about scenarios in which I was the keynote speaker at conferences. The notion that my efforts could have widespread impact motivated me to grow and to pursue excellence in all areas of public service, especially speaking. Over the course of about a decade in my development as a communicator, I watched and listened to innumerable preachers, motivational speakers, comics, news anchors, teachers, and governmental leaders. I trained myself not only to listen to what was being *said*, but to observe what was being *done* by a speaker to move an audience. I believed obtaining access to and properly leveraging platforms would be the most significant factor to maximize my potential.

Twenty years later, my perspective has changed significantly.

What I did not understand during my years of fascination with platforms was the part relationships play in the facilitation of a platform to begin with. In the motivational conference arena, for instance, I did not realize that an event host introducing a guest speaker in a packed-out arena may have had years—even decades—of friendship with the individual about to take the floor. I did not know about the process building up to that very event—the months of conversations, calls, and emails hashing out the details, and ultimately the onsite, last-minute fine tuning, all of which can pose challenges to relationships, while also offering opportunities to go deeper. The magnificence I saw in the platform had overshadowed my estimation of the subtle but essential element of relationship building that takes place at a table.

My friend John Lee says, "Operating from a platform is like spraying water towards a bottle. Only some of the water will enter. A table, however, gives me the opportunity to pour from my bottle right into yours." A multi-millionaire Greek businessman once told me, "I have never once closed a deal in my office. It was always at a table." Though my friend and his clients eventually went to the office to sign paperwork, he said, "The deal was often sealed over a steak." Anything that happens on a platform originates from or leads to a table.

While I value the broad impact made possible from platforms, for over a decade now I have focused more on the relational and socio-economic factors associated with the facilitation of platforms. I treasure behind-the-scenes relationship-building more than the thrill of the moment or even the end result of a speaking engagement. Moreover, I have come to recognize that platforms can be traps for those motivated by ambition and an insatiable need for affirmation from others. I have committed myself to learning about the code of conduct—or protocol—that must govern our behavior both at tables and on platforms. And I have learned to value the state of hiddenness—a concept we will discuss at length below.

As with any character-building process, I have not had an easy run with this. My erroneous mindsets have been continually challenged. My motives and intentions have undergone Heaven's strict scrutiny. I have worked diligently to improve as a contributor or facilitator on platforms, and more importantly, as a friend and confidant at tables. Through it all, our heavenly Father has kept His finger on me, demanding high standards of excellence.

Amazingly, the more I valued good character, relationships, and the process of hiddenness, the wider my platform became. That proves to me God is not opposed to us having broad-sweeping influence and impact as long as we do everything on His terms and according to His ways. Everyone has a measure of influence. Influence is the capacity to make our lives appealing enough to others, to the point where they invite us in to share their journey, to speak into their world, and ultimately to impact their lives. People watch, hear, and continually evaluate us. Our individual gifts and callings may usher us into the platforms of the public arena or into the confines of intimate gatherings around tables. In either case, the gauge of our influence hinges significantly on our character—the part of us that develops, not on a stage under a spotlight, but in the most private place, the state of being found in the hidden place.

I submit this book to you as a collection of excerpts from my journey from platforms to tables and vice versa. I offer insight as your fellow-student in the subject, not as a teacher or an expert. These are my notes thus far, and I hope you glean something from them.

# TABLES & PLATFORMS

# CHAPTER 1

# The State of Hiddenness

SOME YEARS AGO, I was invited to join an international team of ministers in a developing nation. Our assignment was to teach pastors and leaders about the ways of God's Kingdom as they pertained to finance. The event organizer was a well-known influencer in that region and his invitation by phone was personal and encouraging. He asked me to fund my own trip as this was "missions." I gladly agreed. Though being asked to participate was an honor, various aspects of the conference made me feel as though I was the new kid on the block who had not really arrived yet.

At the conference center, I began to experience some of the negative dynamics often associated with large platforms. The arena was packed with people and scores more were still making their way into the building. One after another, sedans and vans dropped off speakers near the front entrance. That scene would have been enticing during my days of dreaming about big platforms, but being in it was a different story altogether.

We were ushered into a "prayer room," where we met the organizers and embarked on introductions. The room was full of awkwardness and tension, as numerous speakers meeting each other for the first time were trying to make the best of their brief acquaintance just minutes before we all had to march out onto a large stage. The absence of relationship created a void that no high calling, noble cause, or eloquent preaching could ever fill.

And yet, even during those strange first moments, the hosts gave me the great honor of receiving the only offering that would be taken up at the conference. The offering would be received after my session—the afternoon session, that is.

Here's a large-stage unspoken secret: Morning and evening sessions are for the star speakers, while the afternoon sessions are for—well, I think you understand. I have affectionately referred to the session after lunch as the graveyard shift. Generally, by that time excitement from the morning session has worn off and the high-carb lunches attendees have just ingested cause them to be sleepy. As a speaker, you pour your life into that afternoon speaking session, and some people sleep through it. Worse yet, the other speakers, and especially the hosts, are frequently nowhere to be seen. They are having coffee while hanging out in the prayer room. In this case, they did make a grand entrance at the end of my message, as we were receiving the offering at that time.

Back in the prayer room, the conference hosts had said, "You are going to take the offering, Marios. We need eighty thousand dollars. You have the session after lunch. Brother, you carry breakthrough—bring it!" But what they were really saying was, "That session is the worst—we do not want it. We are not even going to be in the room until you've done your thing. Then we'll sneak in for *our* thing."

I knew exactly what was going on. Two star speakers would inspire the audience with magnificent morning sessions. They would help set the right atmosphere. The people would be prepared to respond spiritually and, ultimately, financially. Not that the event was about money—it wasn't—but there was undoubtedly strategy involved in how the financial part would play out.

I had been asked to receive the large offering because they believed I could leverage the grace on my life to compel people to give. They had heard of such things happening in my ministry before, so they were tapping into my anointing and authority to receive offerings. It was true—I was gifted with grace for offerings, but not because of anything I've ever done publicly. Rather, the grace for that and every assignment comes from what happens in my secret place. I call it the realm of hiddenness.

---

Everyone I share my life with as a close confidant or mentor will attest to my fascination with and desire for hiddenness—the state of being in which one establishes identity and finds affirmation in his/her relationship with God.

The *hidden place* is not a physical location: it is a state of being. It is the internal dimension where we simply *are* and *become*. *"If a ruler listens to lies, all his servants will be wicked"* (Proverbs 29:12 TLV). The verse speaks of a kingdom where a ruler who pays attention to lies establishes an environment out of which every servant in that kingdom becomes wicked, which means that they were not wicked to begin with. Through the process of that king engaging lies, they became wicked. Jesus said to His disciples, *"...Follow Me, and I will make you fishers of men"* (Matthew 4:19 NKJV). None of them were fishers of men when Jesus made the invitation, but in the process of being with Jesus, they could become something they were not. The Lord established an environment out of which eleven would change the world, even if one betrayed Him. Everyone is born with destiny, within an environment. Our environment will have a significant role in what we may become. The realm of hiddenness is the perfect environment for us to become what we were always destined to be.

Hiddenness is where we are 100% who the Father knows us to be. It is not a front we put on when we are with other people or the games we play as we vie for position. It is just us and Him. The hidden place gives us space to vent and room to grow. There, our shortcomings are exposed, and through our Father's love, we have an opportunity to come to terms with them and improve. By the same token, our strengths and accomplishments are affirmed and celebrated by our Creator, safely, without strings attached. There, our successes are not exploited for someone else's gain. In the hidden place, Yahweh corrects us, commends us and encourages us to go on.

(Yahweh is the English transliteration of the Hebrew name for God, from the Hebrew letters Yod, Hey, Vav, Hey, or YHVH.)

Due to my having undergone a heavenly-prescribed process of dying to self, the leaders of the conference noticed fruit in my life. They saw fruit because I had been thriving in the hidden place. Jesus said, *"You will know them by their fruits"* (Matthew 7:16 NKJV). Dedication to the processes of transformation I underwent in the hidden place released abundance for my work, and financial resources followed me in my pursuits. I had come out of the place where I had been stripped of everything, and I did so gladly. When we come out of the hidden place into the place of generosity that the Father builds in our hearts, we become givers. My authority to receive an offering on that particular assignment, and everywhere, did not come from being a leader of a church or a preacher on an international platform. It came from being a giver in the secret place. It came from establishing systems of generosity that only my heavenly Father and my wife know about.

The hidden place, that state of being, is where I resort to in moments like the one I was experiencing at the conference in that developing country. The only way I can carry out my assignment in a setting where conference agendas and pecking orders supersede genuine, pure Kingdom friendship and camaraderie is to block out all noise and go deeper into the heart of my Father.

I go to that hidden place when I am around arrogant people who like to brag about their status and accomplishments. When you first meet them, they tell you their résumé, highlighting how much greater they are than you, showcasing all their successes. The problem? Everything revolves around what they have done, not about who they are and what they are becoming. When I am in the company of such individuals, I immediately enter into hiddenness. While they carry on about all their great exploits, what they've done that I have not, I am not even present any more. My body may be in front of them, my head nodding and my face smiling, but who I really am in God is in the secret place with Him.

> *The hidden place is a state of being and the internal dimension where we are and become who God created us to be.*

In the hidden place, I hang around with my heavenly tutors. Let me explain this by briefly delving into the more mystical part of my walk with God. I came to Christ by encountering Yahweh in a dream. He introduced Himself to me and I surrendered my life to Him. I was *saved* in that dream. When I awoke, I was not the same person. I had made a commitment to follow Jesus. Since then, I have built much of my spiritual life on similar mystical encounters, of which I only speak in settings conducive to such talk. Among other encounters, I have been aware of a delegation system in Heaven, whereby God assigns our training and equipping to other beings or entities, such as the Seven Spirits of God. In other words, my discipleship as a son has not been directly from the Father, though all credit and glory for any advancement is His. Yahweh has assigned heavenly mentors and guides, among whom have been the persons of Honor, Favor, and the Spirit of Wisdom, who, according to the Bible, had an integral part in creation and walks closely with Yahweh as well as with all His sons who will heed her voice (see especially Proverbs 1, 4, and 8). I have also been tutored by several biblical characters in the heavenly places where I've met them, including King Solomon, whom I've encountered both as the king of the books of Kings and Chronicles and as the preacher of Ecclesiastes. Most of my encounters take place when I choose hiddenness. So, while someone blathers on about how great he/she is, I choose to ascend to the hidden place and seek the camaraderie and instruction of my tutors.

I have also learned to go into that place when I am accused. Accusation is a vicious foe, and one that can never be beaten if we respond with the same spirit the accusation came with. We must remember that we are of a different spirit. Our spirit is cultivated in the hidden place, not on the battlefield where the enemy wants us to fight on their terms. Silence is one of the most powerful weapons we can use against accusation—silence in the presence of the Lord, that is. Psalm 62:1 says, *"Truly, my soul silently waits for God; From Him comes my salvation"* (NKJV). We all know when an accusation is 100% false, and we are completely innocent; we also know when there may be a hint of truth in it. The hidden place is where we sort it out—with God. We must not respond defensively and engage in earthly battles with earthly means.

Hiddenness is also what I seek when I am challenged by greatness, such as when I face a feat or person that raises the bar in terms of achievement and/or character. In such moments I feel as though a strong wind blows through my being, challenging what has been established within me already, and I have to re-evaluate and perhaps amend my ways.

I experienced something of this nature one night in Singapore, when after a full day of conference meetings, a spiritual dimension opened up to me. I stepped into it by faith even though I did not understand it all. At about 3:00 A.M., while asleep, I had an encounter with Mr. Lee Kuan Yew, the first Prime Minister of modern-day Singapore. Under Mr. Lee, the nation went from being comprised of mud huts and fishing villages to its current status as a first-world nation. Singapore became the number one place to do business, according to *Economist* magazine in 2015, all in one generation.[1] That sort of meteoric rise has never before happened. That a nation can go from nothing to greatness because of one man and his leadership is astounding. It happened with Mr. Lee Kuan Yew, and I encountered that man and his legacy in a heavenly realm in the middle of the night in Singapore.

Everything done in Singapore is done with excellence and integrity. During my numerous visits to Singapore, there have been several times when I saw people carrying large sums of cash in different currencies up to bank tellers. They brought the money to the bank themselves, in duffel bags, with no hired security, no armed guards. One can wire money anywhere in the world from Singaporean banks in just a few minutes because of the efficiency of its bank clerks as well as its supervisors who hover over the clerks to ensure that everything is done correctly.

In Singapore, the streets are safe and the spiritual atmosphere is clean and open. You can be fined for jay-walking or for chewing gum and spitting it on the ground. There is barely any crime in the nation. There is a high standard of uprightness because Mr. Lee and his administration engaged with and applied a blueprint from Heaven for their nation.

---

[1] "Why Singapore Became an Economic Success." The Economist. March 26, 2015. Accessed July 24, 2019. https://www.economist.com/the-economist-explains/2015/03/26/why-singapore-became-an-economic-success.

So, I encountered Mr. Lee in my sleep and then woke up and began to research about him. I started by watching Mr. Lee's funeral, which had taken place about a month earlier that year. I began to understand what was being said about him, as I read and watched his speeches. Margaret Thatcher once said, "Prime Minister, an hour's talk with you is itself worth a journey halfway round the world and further still," at a banquet Mr. Lee once held in her honor.[2]

When I encounter that sort of level of greatness, there is only one place for me to go next: the hidden place where I can be further-tutored and trained. I want what I encountered in Singapore for my nation; I want that for every nation I walk in. I want to impart those principles from the platform God has given me. When we are challenged by greatness, we must not allow insecurity to set in, causing us to criticize ourselves for what we have not yet attained. Instead, we must seek to rise to that level. We must become willing to pay the price to ascend, to go deeper, to grow.

Hiddenness is the state in which inspiration can go to work and produce the best fruit. Inspiration activates the greatness that is within us, in order to align us with the purpose for which we exist. Inspiration is the catalyst for change in our lives. When we are inspired, the Holy Spirit has the reins of our hearts, and He can guide us in the paths of righteousness. Inspiration is the great motivator that pushes us beyond the confines of limitation and the boundaries of mediocrity. While in the secret place, inspiration grows and develops, it gets tested, and it matures. In hiddenness, we have the best chance to achieve and become whatever we envision in the moments when we are inspired.

2 "Speech at Official Banquet in Singapore," April 8, 1985, Margaret Thatcher Foundation. Accessed July 19, 2019. https://www.margaretthatcher.org/document/106017.

I'd like to end this chapter with another thought: On tables and platforms alike, when we choose hiddenness as our primary state of being, those who have a similar value system will recognize us. In a way, the light that shines on us when we are in the state of hiddenness shines much brighter than any light we can shine on ourselves or than the glow emanating from those we may choose to get close to so we may shine, too.

Not long ago, I was in a situation where a notable leader and I ended up in the same car, heading to the same hotel. The leader was coming to speak at a conference. Due to my relationship with the organizers of the conference, and particularly because of a series of meetings that were taking place before the conference, I was there at the same time as this leader. Due to his notoriety and especially because he was the keynote speaker at the event, he was the center of attention at a small group gathering that took place before our car ride to the hotel.

I knew much of the leader's legacy, and I had met him once before briefly. I had much respect for him. His talk was inspiring. I was impressed with what he carried. But as I said earlier, high-level inspiration drives me into the state of hiddenness, not self-promotion or attention seeking. I generally avoided contact with this man, and I was happy to simply enjoy the refreshments and talk with my friends. But at the end of the evening, the leader and I ended up in the same car for an hour-long drive to our hotel.

During the drive he asked me an insightful question: "Marios, in your work with leaders, what is one conclusion you have come to regarding good leadership? What constitutes good leadership?" It was the type of question that cuts to the chase and puts you on the spot. Your answer demonstrates the level of maturity you have attained in a certain area. In this case for me, it was the subject of leadership.

I had been hidden all day. I had spent time with my Father in the secret place. Unbeknownst to me, there had been a heavenly deposit in my life about this very topic. Without even thinking, I opened my mouth and responded: "Good leaders are those who find the balance between absolutely *not* caring what the people think and absolutely *caring* about what the people think."

There was a long pause from the leader. Then he asked, "Can you elaborate?"

"Yes. Not caring what people think has to do with us finding our affirmation, direction and value in our relationship with God alone. Caring about what the people think has to do with establishing an environment of interdependence within the body, wherein we need and value everyone, and we esteem each person's contribution to the whole. We must be built up on the inside by God, and we must rely on our co-laborers working alongside us for the execution of the assignments for which we are responsible."

The leader laughed with satisfaction. "Marios, can we have dinner together?"

> Good leaders find the balance
> between absolutely not caring what the people think
> and absolutely caring what the people think.

After almost three hours at dinner, we agreed to have breakfast in the morning. During much of the time we spent together, he and I went deeper in the very subject that had opened up during the previous night's ride to the hotel. More great things have come out of our relationship, but suffice it to say that when we choose to live and operate out of the realm of hiddenness, those who treasure that place will recognize us and they will value us, sometimes immediately, simply because they too treasure the place where the best development of character takes place.

When I speak at conferences, I often get off-the-record questions like these: "We have never heard of you. Who are you? How come you are speaking here? How are you connected to the organizers and the keynote speakers?" I smile and find something to respond with, but deep down I am very pleased. My plan is working. I continue to be hidden. From that place, I will come forth and make a deposit at the conference. And those who have eyes to see and ears to hear will know where I'm coming from.

Our effectiveness on tables and platforms alike depends on our positioning—not at the tables or the platforms, but in the heavenly realms where our character is tested and built up. That is where our true effectiveness is developed. Learn to love that place; learn to love the state of being called hiddenness.

# CHAPTER 2

# Hiddenness as a Life Cycle

IF I WERE TO LIKEN HIDDENNESS to a live organism, it would have a life cycle comprised of two distinct phases or stages: first of being fully concealed and second of being fully revealed. Unlike an organism that begins in phase 1, grows to phase 2, then dies (story over), the phases of the life cycle of hiddenness are continuous, cyclical, and often overlapping. This chapter will discuss the part of the cycle of hiddenness when we are being concealed; the following chapter will address the dynamics involved with being revealed.

Yeshua demonstrates the phases of the life cycle of hiddenness through His own life on earth, and He demonstrates how we should position ourselves in both phases of that cycle. (*Yeshua* is the English transliteration of Jesus' Hebrew name, from the Hebrew letters Yod, Hey, Shin, Vav, Hey, or YHSVH.) Consider the following examples from the first chapter of the Gospel of Mark.

God announces to all those watching as John baptizes Jesus, *"...'You are my beloved Son, in whom I am well pleased.' Immediately the Spirit drove him [Jesus] into the wilderness..."* (Mark 1:11–12 NKJV).

As Mark tells the story, we see that just as Jesus was fully revealed, He was then fully concealed. The change happened immediately.

Sometimes the transition from being revealed to being concealed takes time, and sometimes it happens immediately. I have frequently stood in front of leaders of a nation, and then just twenty-four hours later, been on the side of a mountain where we lived at the time, walking my dog and greeting my Russian neighbor as he drove by. We can go from the highest platform to the most obscure place, just like that. We need to know how to remain hidden with Christ in God in both settings.

*"Now in the morning, having risen a long while before daylight, He went out and departed to a solitary place; and there He prayed"* (Mark 1:35 NKJV). This description of Jesus going to a hidden place occurs after He had healed everyone and delivered everybody of demons outside of Peter's mother-in-law's house. Yeshua healed everyone: he had one hundred percent success. Most would have put a tent up right then and there and held a revival for weeks because the results were good and the offerings (I am sure) were great. But after holding a powerful meeting with awesome results, Jesus went into a solitary place. He was fully revealed, then fully concealed.

Simon and the others with Jesus searched for Him. When they found Him, they said, *"Everyone is looking for you"* (Mark 1:37 NKJV). Jesus' response was, *"...Let us go into the next towns, that I may preach there also..."* (Mark 1:38 NKJV). So again, after being concealed, He was fully revealed.

After healing a leper, we learn that Jesus:

> *...strictly warned him and sent him away at once, and said to him, "See that you say nothing to anyone; but go your way, show yourself to the priest, and offer for your cleansing those things which Moses commanded, as a testimony to them." However, he went out and began to proclaim it freely, and to spread the matter, so that Jesus could no longer openly enter the city, but was outside*

*in deserted places; and they came to Him from every direction.* (Mark 1:43–45 NKJV)

*"Say nothing to anyone,"* Jesus directed. But while Jesus sought full concealment, the healed man fully exposed Jesus to everyone. In that region, before phones, before television, before mass communication, word spread quickly because true greatness was in Israel. True greatness was before them in the form of amazing revelation, extraordinary gifting, and miraculous power from Heaven, all present in the character of the man able to hold up under the weight of that glory. When people see something like that, you cannot stop them from spreading the word: they will talk. The Son of God failed at nothing. While He never failed, the Bible indicates that He could not stop people from telling everyone, even when He warned them not to. True greatness is powerful. If you carry it, you are unstoppable. You do not have to promote yourself. Your anointing will do the work for you.

> *True greatness is powerful. If you carry it, you are unstoppable. You do not have to promote yourself. Your anointing will do the work for you.*

Being fully concealed and fully revealed is not a linear process. It is a cyclical process. It happens again and again, over and over. Through the cycles you are covered in the realm of hiddenness, which, again, is a state of being. Regardless of whether people are watching you, celebrating you, shouting you down, or hating you and pushing you into the desert, you have to make the choice to go in with the Father. No outside opinion matters when you are in Him.

What happens between episodes of being fully concealed and fully revealed is *process*. Often, process is painful. But we have to learn to value process because going through process prepares us for what lies ahead.

I often refer to my Special Forces training in my speaking engagements. Though it took place a long time ago, my experiences from that training regimen are still vivid. One of the most remarkable elements of Green Beret boot camp is that every exercise is strategically chosen because of the way it connects to a bigger picture. For example, the attention to detail our instructors relentlessly insisted upon regarding the care of our personal effects and our sleeping quarters came in handy when the complexity of our training increased, and we were given responsibility over weapons and other equipment critical for our mission. The initially painstaking process of boot camp made more sense to us as we progressed in our development as warriors. The same pattern applies to our walk with God. A difficult process *now* has the potential to equip us with authority and character for future tasks.

The spotlight that shines on you when you are center stage never shines on the rocky path it took to get there.[3] When the referee lifts the hand of the boxer who won the match, with the crowd cheering in the background, no one announces how many hours he spent in a musty gym—no one cheered then. When a tear falls from the eye of the gold medalist at the Olympics, it is not because of her flag that is being raised and the crowd's applause. No. The tear holds all the pain it took the athlete to get to that place. The tear falls because she was injured numerous times and it looked impossible to qualify for the Olympics, but somehow she got there and somehow she won.

---

[3] I have written on this previously in *Weaponized Honor* (Sound of Thunder Publications, 2017). There I stated it this way: "The spotlight that shines on us, on life's platform, never shines on the rocky paths we must first traverse to get there." (19).

When we are fully concealed, we risk wanting to be revealed prematurely. There are two challenges in a concealed phase. The first challenge comes when we know there is greatness within us, and we have the desire to serve our Father now. But we must undergo process, and because we are tempted to jump the gun to serve or be in the spotlight now, process is hard. We may be tempted to act as Abraham did with Sarah's servant. Abraham procured the son he'd been promised by doing things Abraham's way—he leaned on the arm of the flesh. But we must resist jumping the gun. We have to endure and even appreciate the process God takes us through.

As an example of the process one might need to go through in a concealed phase, consider what it would be like to be invited to speak at your first conference. Wow, you might think, I'm being revealed! But are you? Somebody said to somebody else, "You should have her/him speak," but you are given the afternoon shift. This small detail may tell you that you are indeed still fully concealed.

They will say, "Come." You see them as they strut to where they are sitting down. They have a person whose job is to remove lint from their jacket, a person who drives them everywhere, and another person who cuts their meat for them. They strut themselves about, they have invited you, and then they do not even sit and listen to you speak.

> *The spotlight that shines on you when you are center stage never shines on the rocky path it took to get there.*

What do you do in response? Dial down. Remain fully concealed to let greatness percolate in you. Let the Father do the work while you stay hidden. They may leave your name off the program. They may forget to even mention you as they list the conference speakers on opening night. Just dial down. Yes: it may hurt, but resist the temptation to demand attention for yourself.

While fully concealed, we must resist the urge to be revealed. The desire to be recognized, to be known, is why in numerous countries around the world, people have fifty ways to post videos of themselves. Not just selfies, but constant "Look at me!" videos. Society is becoming inundated with them and people are getting fed up with this narcissistic focus. The deep is calling unto deep and people are starting to ask, "Where are the hidden ones, where do we find them?"

The question brings us to another dynamic associated with hiddenness—that of hidden ones being drawn to other hidden ones.

A dear friend of mine from Singapore, Watchman Ngiam (his real name), has walked around the entire nation of Singapore more than a dozen times. If God says to him, "Walk around Singapore," he walks around the entire country. According to the divine instruction he has received, Watchman straps two flags on his back—one red and one white, representing the blood of Jesus and purity. And he walks, completely unphased by the looks of surprise or disdain of motorists and others. Once his wife was going to work and a lady next to her on the bus said, "Look at that weird guy." Watchman's wife said, "That is my husband, actually!"

Once during his walks, Watchman walked into a building, went up to an executive in that establishment and said, "You are about to become the top leader." He prophesied over that individual and it all came true. In obedience to God's directives, my friend had similar uncomfortable, yet impact-filled messages for other significant leaders in his nation. As a result, Watchman obtained instant credibility with individuals. I have ministered at his house numerous times, where it is not uncommon to have wealthy and influential people from all walks of life sit at his feet to learn. His submission to the process of hiddenness has produced a greatness that the great are drawn to.

It was in the throes of intense process during one of my seasons of concealment years ago that I met Watchman Ngiam. There was an instant connection between us. When circumstances beyond my control had caused the cancellation of a speaker for a major event, immediately, though I had only known this brother for just a few hours, I asked him to fill in. He did! Then he opened up his platform to me—the nation of Singapore. Neither of our lives have been the same since. Sometimes when people ask me how this opportunity came about, I explain, "My wife Danielle says, 'The more hidden we are, the more He notices us.' Singapore opened up to me and America to my Singaporean friend, because Heaven noted the hidden ones and arranged for us to connect."

Greatness will manifest, if not immediately, then eventually. Greatness will rise up and it will flow out—it is unstoppable. If you will stay hidden and not worry about promoting yourself and getting yourself out there, God will connect you with other hidden ones. In my travels, I have observed that people are generally fed up with self-promoters. They desire to find the hidden ones who carry true greatness, who house true substance from Heaven. So, if people say to you, "I have never heard of you," think to yourself, "Yes! Yes! It is working!"

---

The second challenge is to remain fully hidden when you are fully revealed. When you love what happens in the hidden place, you want to stay there.

In some ways I find being fully revealed to be a sacrifice, because I love the mountain of concealment where nobody knows me, that mountain where there is just me and my Father, and we are okay. I prefer the fully concealed stage of hiddenness over the fully revealed stage of holding a microphone in front of audiences, whether large or small.

When, due to calling and assignment from Heaven, I am to come out of concealment, I much prefer tables over platforms. It is much easier to remain in the hidden realm at tables than at platforms. And yet, due to the strategic importance of the table meeting (who is present, the matters at hand, the potential in the relationships, etc.), often it is at a table where Heaven's strongest spotlight may shine on us.

# CHAPTER 3

# From Concealed to Revealed

HIDDENNESS IS IN MANY WAYS A REFINING PROCESS. Our credibility and influence in the world hinges on how we handle the process of being hidden—especially during a concealed phase. But once that concealed phase is completed, and we fare well through its process, the next phase emerges—revealing. Our posture in this phase must be one of rest, not striving. As stated earlier, we must not rush the process to be revealed. When that phase commences, it must not be the result of self-promotion. Rather, it should be a natural product of others recognizing the substance in us. Stated simply, going from concealed to revealed must not be driven by our ambition or zeal and it should involve input from those around us. Often, that recognition is in direct proportion to our attitude while we are concealed and the process we submit to between the two phases.

The process we undergo with God is a refining process. It's not unlike the process raw gold and silver are put through to purify them: *"The refining pot is for silver and the furnace for gold. And a man is valued by what others say of him"* (Proverbs 27:21 NKJV).

The quality of gold and silver, and hence their value, is determined by how they emerge from a process that involves being subjected to intense heat—the refining pot and furnace. In other words, gold and silver's worth depends on what the fire will "say of them" after they undergo the refining process. It is the same with us—our worth is best established by what others say of us, not by our self-affirmation and posturing for positions of influence. We see the advice in Proverbs: *"Let another man praise you, and not your own mouth; A stranger, and not your own lips"* (27:2 NKJV).

I once spent a considerable amount of time with a very wealthy and influential couple. We drove in their car all day visiting various sites on a Greek island in the Mediterranean. At the end of the day, and after numerous inspiring conversations, the woman of the house asked me this question:

"Marios, what is the largest donation you have ever received for your church and/or humanitarian work?" And just like that, I was faced with a cut-to-the-chase question by someone who possessed much insight and understanding. My answer would immediately communicate to her the value others place on my work. In essence, through her question, the wise woman was saying, "I've been hearing you all day and I like what I'm hearing. But what are others saying about you—especially through resources they direct towards your endeavors?"

Herein lies a major difference between the two phases of hiddenness: when we are concealed, the people around us have no input; but the opposite is the case when we are revealed—people notice something of value in us, and they affirm us with their words and actions.

In the concealed phase of hiddenness, we are not celebrated. It is a place where no one is clapping. It is a place where most of the time nobody is even looking. No one cares. No one was aware of Paul in the desert for three years. No one noted Moses when he tended sheep on the backside of the desert for forty years. Similarly, no one seemed to care about David either.

They did not even bring him in when Samuel arrived in Bethlehem to anoint one of Jesse's sons to be the next king. But in time, everything changed and these heroes of our faith were later revealed: Paul became one of the greatest early Christian fathers and wrote much of what constitutes the New Testament; Moses led the entire nation out of Egypt and through the desert; and David reigned for forty years in Israel, leaving a legacy of government and uprightness that is celebrated to this day.

We must always be mindful of the fact that from Heaven's perspective we are being evaluated continually. Both the concealed and revealed phases of hiddenness are a time of testing, but in different ways. In my experience, the chances of failing are much greater when people are fully revealed than when they are concealed. I have seen very few people make grievous, deal-breaking mistakes while concealed, but I have witnessed the demise of many who were riding high on a wave of success and prominence. Our character is tested the most during the times when we are revealed. It is after proving ourselves in those seasons that we are *"valued by what others say of [us]"*.

---

Many desire and pursue the fame and influence that accompany being revealed without first understanding that such privilege demands responsibility. The higher we ascend on the professional, socio-economic, or even geopolitical ladder, the greater the responsibility. I once met with a friend who is a wealthy business owner for dinner, and his story demonstrates the heavy responsibilities that can accompany privilege. We ate at an outstanding restaurant. We both happened to order steak. When our meals arrived, my friend was sharing some of the professional challenges he was facing. One of his factories had experienced setbacks. He had to lay off some of his workers— men and women he considered family due to their longevity with the company. A manager in another complex was controlling and difficult to work with. A family member whom he had appointed as CEO of one of his companies was going through severe personal problems.

Knowing my friend's vast reach and great wealth, and judging by the very things he was wearing, the car he drove to the meeting, etc., I would have thought he was continually enjoying the greatest life imaginable: houses on the beach, hot tubs, jet skis, boats, a fleet of cars, a massive residence in the woods, and much more. Yet there he was, pouring out his heart about the troubled waters he was navigating.

Our waiter arrived with the steaks and set them before us. My friend looked at me. As though he could read my mind, he said, "I know it's hard for you to imagine a man like me having problems." Pausing, he looked down at his plate. He pointed at its contents and said, "Marios, no matter how much money I have, I can only eat one steak at a time, but my level of responsibility increases almost daily."

The concealed phase of hiddenness requires us to be responsible to maintain a heart of humility and fervency before Yahweh, without desiring all the benefits that relationship can procure for us. Being revealed makes us responsible to those around us—family, employees, employers, the people who helped us get there, and all who may be inspired by our example.

———

Being revealed does not only elicit the admiration and appreciation one might expect. Often, it makes us the target of opposition, even persecution. In Acts chapter five, we read about how some of the disciples of Jesus had been thrown in prison and knocked around. The authorities—the Pharisees, scribes, elders, and teachers of the law—had beaten the disciples and were deciding whether or not to execute them.

At the same time, someone else came into the picture—an influential man who had been observing the revealing of Christ's disciples: *"... [A] Pharisee named Gamaliel, a noted religious professor who was highly respected by all, stood up. He gave orders to send the apostles outside"* (Acts 5:34 TPT). Gamaliel was notable as a Pharisee because the people respected him. People did not generally respect the Pharisees. That is why Mark specifies when Jesus came on the scene, He *"taught them as one having authority, and not as the scribes"* (Mark 1:22 NKJV). They found in Jesus what they always hoped would show up: true greatness. Until then, all they had seen was counterfeit greatness: those who paraded in the marketplace, put on robes and phylacteries, and took widows' houses. All they had ever seen was a form of godliness that denied its true power. Therefore, when a leader possessing true greatness showed up, people were drawn to Him.

Gamaliel, though a Pharisee, was one such leader. He was respected by all people. The moment he opened his mouth, everyone listened. When Gamaliel commanded the other Pharisees who were plotting to kill the apostles to put them out of the room for a little while, the Pharisees obeyed.

Gamaliel said:

> *Men of Israel, take heed to yourselves what you intend to do regarding these men. For some time ago Theudas rose up, claiming to be somebody. A number of men, about four hundred, joined him. He was slain, and all who obeyed him were scattered and came to nothing. After this man, Judas of Galilee rose up in the days of the census, and drew away many people after him. He also perished, and all who obeyed him were dispersed. And now I say to you, keep away from these men and let them alone; for if this plan or this work is of men, it will come to nothing; but if it is of God, you cannot overthrow it—lest you even be found to fight against God.* (Acts 5:35–39 NKJV)

Gamaliel saw something in the disciples' lives. He watched them before he spoke about them. Gamaliel had observed the followers of Christ and had seen the effects of their ministry. He also took note of the way the disciples carried themselves. He saw that they were not about the dead laws that the rest of the Pharisees had always emphasized. He saw people being healed and people being raised from the dead. He saw it because perhaps he too lived in that place, and he too died in that place —the realm of hiddenness. Gamaliel's example shows that we should always watch, observe and do our research before we speak against anyone, especially publicly.

> *Hiddenness thrusts us*
> *into the heart of God.*

Gamaliel started to realize that there might be a correlation. There might be something about the disciples that was also in him. They could be the "hidden ones," and if so, then the religious establishment was treading on treacherous ground. Moreover, Gamaliel had also seen how things panned out in past history. He noted how impostors could rise up, attract followers and have big gatherings. Similarly, we now see people rise up and become instant celebrities, especially on social media. You can become "somebody" overnight. This obsession is so prevalent in our culture, that children, who years ago dreamed big dreams of being teachers, doctors and nurses, astronauts, now dream of being YouTube stars. Young people often come to me and share dreams of creating videos that "go viral." I say to them, "This is what you are living for—videos that go viral?" The worst thing that could happen is that they get what they want, because if they live for celebrity and do not have the wisdom, character, or the stature to stand up to the weight and responsibility of that kind of exposure, over time they will fall. Self-promotion sits behind such aspirations, just as there was in this sect of Pharisees. As Gamaliel pointed out, Theudas and Judas of Galilee gathered a group of people just like themselves. They all came together, promoted each other, but then the leaders of those movements fell and their work was engulfed into socio-economic black holes of obscurity.

Obscurity can become the end result of a pursuit of greatness when we don't learn to operate in hiddenness. Hiddenness thrusts us into the heart of God and we come out of it having been impacted by what exists in the realm of Heaven. Obscurity is the product of trying to make a name for ourselves *by* ourselves, of placing faith and trust in people who sing our praises because we give them what they want for a season. But eventually, such individuals' lack of character and substance will expose the ephemeral nature of any accomplishment gained through self-promotion. To Gamaliel, the disciples seemed to have come out of the hidden place, and if so, no one should raise a voice or a hand against them. Therefore he admonished, *"Let them alone"* (Acts 5:38). Gamaliel seems to have known that if they were not operating from hiddenness and they were left alone, God would deal with them, and they would end up in obscurity.

---

There is an aspect of hiddenness I wish I could shout from the rooftops: hiddenness costs something. Ultimately it costs us our lives, because hiddenness is about dying to self. Those who learn to be hidden are those who learn how to die. As Paul said, *"Set your mind on things above, not on things on the earth. For you died, and your life is hidden with Christ in God"* (Col. 3:2–3 NKJV). We are not alive any more. We died. The life that we think we now have is actually hidden in heavenly realms, with Christ in God. It is there that Heaven makes rich deposits in our lives so that when we come out, we actually have something to give, something to contribute, something to proclaim, and something to transform.

As I travel the nations, I see it happening. What I am seeing is just the tip of the iceberg, but the face of that iceberg is transformation happening on an international level. There are shakings and stirrings because God is connecting those willing to die with those looking for change. I am not just talking about zealous conference junkies or even regular church-goers. I am talking about people of significant notoriety and achievement from many fields of endeavor, who are inviting those of us who have spent time in the hidden place to sit at their tables and stand on their platforms. They are saying, "Speak to us. We tried everything we know, and it is not working. But there is something we notice in you." Though they cannot describe the *something* they see, what they notice is the product of death to self, death to selfish motives, death to agendas and attitudes.

So, to be able to deal with scenarios like this, we go into the hidden place. It is from the hidden place that I write this book. I remain in that place continually. If we are fascinated with what we need to do, with the call of God on our lives, or with our giftings or talents, but we do not learn how to operate from the place of hiddenness in those things, we will not handle them well. We will be running after the accolades of men, hoping that somebody shakes our hand and tells us we did a good job.

---

The apostles faced opposition and persecution, and we too may face the reproach of those who do not want change. Often, those who most vehemently resist change are not positioned in the halls of power or in the marketplace. They are in churches. The opposition to what we are doing has rarely if ever come from kings and rulers—on the contrary, they love us. Opposition comes from ill-informed and ill-disposed individuals within the body of Christ. Before we confront resistance from religiosity and the political spirit that is prevalent in many church environments, it is crucial to be in the right place inside ourselves. If we deal with opposition out of a place of hurt and woundedness, then we will be limited in our ability to bring transformation. Publicly confronting matters from a place of brokenness leads to a path that is not good, and a destination that is even worse.

True greatness does not move unhindered. As Jesus said, *"...If they persecuted Me, they will persecute you also [...] because they do not know the One who sent Me"* (John 15:20–21 TLV). If we carry true greatness, we will have stuff flying at us—flak, bullets, maybe even missiles.

To that end, Jesus has a word.

> *"It is not what goes into the mouth of a man that defiles and dishonors him, but what comes out of the mouth, this defiles and dishonors him." Then the disciples came and said to Jesus, "Do You know that the Pharisees were offended when they heard you say this?" He answered, "Every plant which My heavenly Father did not plant will be torn up by the roots. Leave them alone; they are blind guides [leading blind followers]. If a blind man leads a blind man, both will fall into a pit."* (Matthew 15:11–14 AMP)

We see another "Let them alone" here. Gamaliel's "Let them alone" addresses not trying to control those who may be working from the hidden, holy place. Jesus' "Leave them alone" expands the concept. Instead of being concerned about what the Pharisees thought, instead of trying to change His message so they wouldn't take offense, instead of attacking back, Yeshua told the disciples to leave them alone. They will expose themselves in due time. Jesus' "Leave them alone" came from knowing the enemies of the Gospel had no case and would not prevail. The same admonition from Gamaliel came from his knowing, deep down, that what the disciples of Jesus carried and did was genuinely from God.

In our church, we have taught a "Leave us alone" message for years. We say, "Let people go through their process. Let each person encounter the discipline and instruction of the Father and stop trying to change everyone. Stop insisting on how others should act or what they should do. Leave them alone. Love them and let God deal with them."

Over the years we received a number of emails from people who do not agree with us. They often start with, "We have some concerns about things…" Rarely, if ever, have such emails been constructive: in fact, they have always been hurtful to those of us in leadership who are pursuing the Kingdom, and who genuinely and passionately love God and serve the body of Christ. One day, I met with our church administrator in my office and said, "We are going to direct all emails 'of concern' to you, and we ask you to take care of them. Any legitimate issues, please bring to our attention; the rest—well, you know what to do." To this day, after more than eight years, I have never seen any of the "concerns" emails. I salute our administrator for doing what he does with them. The leadership of our church is accountable for everything we are and do—but not to individuals who pop in for a Sunday or two and then want to give us a piece of their mind regarding church policy and doctrine. No. Leave us alone.

Anyone with concerns should practice tree-watching. To tree watch, look for the fruit. It's simple: good trees produce good fruit. Those trees can be left alone. Bad trees with no fruit will be taken down by their owners, so leave those alone, too—to God.

Jesus said,

> In the same way, every good [healthy; sound] tree produces good fruit, but a bad [rotten; diseased] tree produces bad fruit… (Matthew 7:17 EXB)

> I chose you. And I gave you this work: [appointed you] to go and produce fruit, fruit that will last… (John 15:16 EXB)

If there was a way to address all who oppose change and raise their voice or hand against other people's noble pursuits, whether ministry or marketplace endeavors, I would cry out in the words of Gamaliel: "Leave us alone. Leave us alone because there is one thread that runs through all of us, and it is that we died." In dying, we have accessed that place of being hidden with Christ in God, and if we have anything to give, it comes from that place. If we truly have something, and that something is allowed to go through the refining fire of the hidden place, there will be fruit that remains from it. As Jesus said: *"You will know them by their fruits"* (Matthew 7:16 NKJV). If there is fruit, then we can all partake. If we are wrong, let Him deal with us. Then we will go into obscurity and you will never hear from us again.

> *"...[K]eep away from these men and let them alone;*
> *for if this plan or this work is of men, it will come to nothing;*
> *but if it is of God, you cannot overthrow it—*
> *lest you even be found to fight against God." ~Acts 5:38–39*

Yahweh is never pleased with individuals or organizations that interfere with His plans and with His servants who execute Hhis will on the earth. When we are ready to pay the price to do what He said to do, others need to honor us or keep quiet about us, but they must not attack us, lest they find themselves being pitted against God.

One day, I returned home from a long and rigorous international ministry assignment. As soon as I had Wi-Fi, up came a message from one of our staff members at the church. "Marios, you will not believe this. There is a guy who posted on Facebook about you using church funds to fly all over the world!" The accusation came at me when I had just arrived home from flying over the Himalayas. I had cried my eyes out on the flight, holding on to the hem of Jesus' garment in the hidden place. I had paid my own way to go on the trip during a time of much financial need at home, and I was coming home with nothing by way of finance. On this, of all days, a man raised his voice against me in that way.

I thanked the staff member for letting me know, but I did absolutely nothing about the malicious post about my travels. I went back into hiddenness, and even while in the presence of God, I said nothing about the matter. I have learned a powerful principle from King David. In Psalm 62:1, which we looked at earlier, David said, *"Truly my soul silently waits for God; From Him comes my salvation"* (NKJV). Then four verses later we read, *"My soul, wait silently for God alone, for my expectation is from Him"* (v. 5). Who spoke to David's soul, commanding it to stay silent and wait for God? David's spirit did. Our spirit is the part of us that is best connected to the heavenly realms we have come from and where, according to Scripture, we have been seated with Christ (Ephesians 2:4–7). David learned to operate out of his spirit, telling his soul—the seat of emotion and thoughts—to stand down and wait for God. In other words, the pressing matters at hand were not to be processed rationally or emotionally—only spiritually.

I have learned that this type of silence is a powerful posture we can have before the Lord. When I am in the secret place with Him, and I choose relationship and intimacy with Him instead of complaining about my accusers and begging for help with my problems—matters which He already knows about anyway—I gain a position of leverage with God. I have His full attention as a son, and from that place I can ask for anything by saying the least.

After days of choosing hiddenness and saying nothing to God at all about the attack on Facebook, I looked up, opened my mouth, and said one word: "Father!" By uttering His name in that way, I did what Peter did when he came out of prison and said, *"...Lord, look on their threats..."* (Acts 4:29 NKJV). The result in Peter's case, after calling on the Father, was that the place where he and the other apostles stood shook.

There is an authority that manifests when we come out of the hidden place and the people who should have left us alone do not. We can say, "Father." We do not have to tangle with them. We do not have to defend ourselves. We do not have to give a dissertation about why we are right and why they are wrong. We silence our mouths, we raise up our hearts, we look our Father in the face and say, "Father!"

I do not know what happened to the man who attacked me on Facebook. I heard he was arrested, then in a half-way house, then moved across the country, then... who knows? All I know is that I left him alone for not leaving me alone, and my Father dealt with the issue.

---

The day I turned forty I went running and I started praying this prayer: "Father, help me to know how much you love me." I did not pray, "Help me to do more stuff for you." It was not about works. I wanted to understand who I am in Him, because He is my Father who really loves me. I have a biological father who showed me nothing but love, so it was easy for me to accept my heavenly Father's love. When you accept His love and know how much you are loved, it changes everything. You treasure the hidden place, because that is where you obtain greater understanding of the facets of Yahweh's love. When you stay in the hidden place, covered by the Father's love, you commit your status in the world and any influence you will have in the earth, no matter whether you are concealed or revealed, fully to His hands. His instruction, direction, affirmation, encouragement and protection are found in *"the secret place of the most High"* (Psalm 91:1 NKJV).

Is there any better place to be?

# CHAPTER 4

# Invites and Intros

LEARNING TO VALUE AND OPERATE FROM the state of hiddenness, in both the concealed and revealed phases, and faring well throughout the process hiddenness demands, will ultimately result in us having greater impact. The only other factor involved is time. That is an element we cannot control, for it exists within the auspices of God's sovereignty. Putting together various concepts we have been exploring, I propose the following: through the development of our character while we grow in relationship with Yahweh, what is deposited in us will manifest and find expression over time, by way of increased substance *in* us and influence *through* us.

For me, influence is like currency in that it affords certain privileges while levying responsibility on those who possess it. Like financial instruments, influence must be obtained (or earned) and it must be stewarded properly. The Bible is replete with advice regarding our posture and behavior in stewarding influence. One of my favorite places to look for such wisdom is in the Book of Proverbs. Consider the following passage:

> *When you sit down to eat with a ruler,*
> *Consider carefully what is before you;*

*And put a knife to your throat*
*If you are a man given to appetite.*
*Do not desire his delicacies,*
*For they are deceptive food.* (Proverbs 23:1–3 NKJV)

The setting laid out by these verses is easy to visualize, but the objective of this exhortation has been grossly misunderstood and misinterpreted. I have heard preachers use the verses as a strong warning against the sin of gluttony and/or the deceptive nature of rulers. Approaching these verses from those angles does not reveal the true reason Solomon shared these words with his son. We must keep in mind that Solomon's original purpose for writing the Proverbs was to instruct his son in the way he should walk.

When a ruler like Solomon instructs his son regarding proper posture when dining with another ruler, gluttony and the exposure of rulers' deceptions are the last things on his mind. He is one of the greatest rulers who has ever walked the planet. He is addressing his son who is in line to succeed him as ruler.

The key to properly interpreting Solomon's words lies with verse 1: *"When you sit down to eat with a ruler…"* Stated a bit differently: "I, Solomon—a ruler—am teaching you, my son— soon to be a ruler—how to behave when you sit down to eat with another ruler. That you are a ruler sitting with another ruler takes preeminence over all other factors at the table, including the food. Focusing on the food would be a mistake. The real value of the meal is in the opportunity to be in an intimate setting—at a table—with a ruler."

The ruler of any nation, kingdom, territory, or realm of influence, be it a prime minister of a country, the chief commissioner of FIFA or the National Football League, the CEO of Adobe, or the president of a multinational bank, is not easily accessible. Limited access, especially in the case of high-profile individuals, is essential for establishing and maintaining value. Generally, someone or something easily accessible by the wider public will not be as esteemed or sought after as items that are rare or individuals who are not as readily available. The basic principle of supply and demand applies. Demand (and price) generally increase when supply is limited or decreases.

Due to the high value of those in positions of authority and power, the opportunity to sit across from a "ruler"—much less to sit at his/her table—is contingent on two factors, both of which must be in place: 1) an introduction and 2) an invitation.

Generally, no one ends up in the presence of a ruler without being invited. Invitations are important, especially from a socio-spiritual perspective. As seen in the Book of Esther, in some ancient cultures, such as that during the time of the Persian Empire, entering the king's court without an invitation could lead to immediate execution.

Equally essential are introductions. Proper introductions can be as significant as an invitation in the facilitation of the initial trust needed to proceed with acquaintance and any subsequent development of a relationship.

Introductions and invitations are contingent upon one main qualifier: substance. The substance of our lives, as perceived by those who may introduce and/or invite us, is comprised of the following components: who we are, what we have accomplished, what we are currently involved with, and what we carry—our personality and behavior which stem from our inner value system and character qualities.

While writing this book, I received a high-level invitation to speak at a function organized by a governmental agency of the United States. The catalyst for the invite was a friend who is influential within the organization. When his superior mentioned the need for a speaker for their event, my friend said, "I know a man who served as a Green Beret in the Greek Special Forces, travels the world speaking at events like ours, wrote many books, and has a solid track record of excellence." The leader of the organization invited me based on the recommendation and subsequent introduction that my friend provided.

Tables and platforms require an invitation. Do not sit at a table you are not invited to. Do not stand on a platform you create for yourself, or on one which somebody else built simply to make yourself look good. There is power in a proper invitation. When someone invites us to a platform, they leverage the essence of what they have and everything that has been given to them. Allow them to say, "I want you to come and partake of this. I want you to stand with me and partner with me in the assignment that I have to impact all this." That is an invitation with power.

If it is a nation, and especially if it is the first time we go in, it should be based on a proper invitation from a proper source, with a proper covering, with a proper assignment, with a proper stature in that place. And we had better follow protocol. You had better go with an invitation and not just put yourself there to take a picture and say, "Look where I am today, my friends! 'Like' me!" I have known people who leave the airport during a layover in that particular city, then they take a picture and post it with commentary that gives the impression they were in that nation on assignment. Why? So people can "like" the picture and perceive them as successful? Can you imagine how Heaven evaluates such behavior?

At a leadership conference once, I heard it said, "If you need them, you can't lead them." If we need the pat on the back, we may be lacking what it takes to have true affirmation not from earth, but from Heaven. I am not interested in people shaking my hand after a meeting. While I appreciate it and I am very gracious about it, I am more interested in receiving a nod from Heaven. It is what Daniel got: "You are loved, Daniel; we really esteem you, Daniel. When you prayed, your prayer got answered right away and Heaven was mobilized on your behalf when you prayed." That is what I am interested in; that is the affirmation I desire.

I admire that the apostle Paul, though he established churches in many different ways and many different places, never pushed himself on the people he was spiritually fathering. He never pushed himself on the houses he had personally labored in and suffered greatly to establish. No: he came by invitation.

In the early church, once the apostolic fathers established sons and put them in place in a faith community, they would not go back to that community unless they were invited. That is a precedent, and it's a model that I want to emulate and live by. Danielle and I have many protégés with whom we have shared our lives and whom we have had a part in establishing on their platforms, whether in the government, the military, in business or in ministry. But without an invitation, Danielle and I will not seek to speak into their lives in the same way we did during previous formative stages.

> *Invitations come when those in authority*
> *recognize what we can bring to them.*

An invitation to a platform is important because when we are invited, those who invite us prepare that platform to receive us and our message. This puts the platform in a position to maximize the potential in us in that place to release what God has put in our hearts for those people.

A scripture passage that has been key to me regarding invitations is this:

> *Do not exalt yourself in the presence of the king,*
> *And do not stand in the place of the great;*
> *For it is better that he say to you, "Come up here,"*
> *Than that you should be put lower in the presence of the prince,*
> *Whom your eyes have seen.* (Proverbs 25:6–7 NKJV)

In other words, kings do not appreciate people who put themselves in front of them in order to exalt themselves in the sight of the king. Jesus said something similar in a parable when He was dining with one of the rulers of the Pharisees on the Sabbath:

> *When you are invited by anyone to a wedding feast, do not sit down in the best place, lest one more honorable than you be invited by him; and he who invited you and him come and say to you, "Give place to this man," and then you begin with shame to take the lowest place. But when you are invited, go and sit down in the lowest place, so that when he who invited you comes he may say to you, "Friend, go up higher." Then you will have glory in the presence of those who sit at the table with you. For whoever exalts himself will be humbled, and he who humbles himself will be exalted.* (Luke 14:8–11 NKJV)

The kings of the earth today are leaders of nations (a president or prime minister), of regions (a governor of a state or province), or any person with a scepter of government, so to speak, in their hands. Or perhaps they are kings in another sense, because the kingdoms of this world are not just nations or political governments. Here is what John heard in Heaven concerning the kingdoms of this world: *"Then the seventh angel sounded: And there were loud voices in heaven, saying, 'The kingdoms of this world have become the kingdoms of our Lord and of His Christ, and He shall reign forever and ever!'"* (Revelation 11:15 NKJV). Here, the *kingdoms of this world* are realms of influence. They are *platforms*. So, Google is a kingdom. Facebook is a kingdom, and other large companies are kingdoms of this world. Military forces are kingdoms.

Keeping that understanding in mind, we need to recognize that we should not exalt ourselves in the presence of kings, no matter what kingdom they represent. Those who hold reins of authority to administrate in various realms of influence should be inviting us on to their platforms because they recognize what is in us. They should want to partner with what is in us so that their platforms will benefit from our lives. That's when invitations come—when those in authority recognize what we can bring to them.

Access, especially to prominent and highly influential individuals and entities, requires a genuine demonstration and manifestation of substance in our lives—the key word here is *genuine*. There are two main areas where we establish credibility: Heaven and earth. Invitations and introductions that grant us access on earth are contingent upon our having credibility in Heaven. Thus, it is essential that what is known about us on earth matches what is known about us in Heaven.

Heaven is not impressed with accomplishments. There is no message, there is no sermon, there is no teaching that I could ever bring that is going to impress Heaven. What impresses Heaven is relationship—a walk with Yahweh that honors His ways and His Kingdom, a walk that matches the image we build for those around us. Our private life, known completely only by God, must match our public life on earth.

In Luke 18 we find the story Jesus told about the Pharisee and the tax collector and the way they prayed. The Pharisee got up and said, "I am so thankful that I am not like the tax collector over there. I give tithes; I give offerings; I honor the traditions—I do all the things well. But I am not like that tax collector. Hear my prayer."

The Pharisee, according to the way Jesus dealt with Pharisees in general, and especially because of the way he prayed, is demonstrating a secret life nothing like his public life. Publicly, he was respected in the marketplace, honored among men, known for being a tither, known for his teachings and for his grand entrances into halls and synagogues.

But his private life—what Heaven knew about him—was very different. We know this because Jesus said to the Pharisees,

> *Woe to you [...], you hypocrites! You are like whitewashed tombs, which look beautiful on the outside but on the inside are*

*full of the bones of the dead and everything unclean. In the same way, on the outside you appear to people as righteous but on the inside you are full of hypocrisy and wickedness.* (Matthew 23:27–28 NIV)

That is what Jesus said. He called them *"a brood of vipers"* (Matthew 12:34) and said they were like the blind leading the blind (Matthew 15:14). Basically He was saying, "What you portray in public does not match who you are in the eyes of God and all of Heaven."

But let's look at the tax collector, whom everyone knew to be vile, corrupt, and crooked. In the secret place, in the private place with God, he says, "I'm a tax collector and I'm a sinner. Have mercy on me!" And what he was in private matched very closely who he was in public. And Heaven said, "We like this guy. Granted!" Heaven wants *real*, and the church desperately cries out for *real*—for those whose lives are the same in private and in public, who have no guile, who have no hidden agendas or hidden motives. Their lives are bare both before the Lord and before those to whom they are accountable.

> Heaven is not impressed with accomplishments.
> What impresses Heaven is relationship—a walk with Yahweh
> that honors His ways and His Kingdom.

It is from that place and with this understanding that I refer to some things that Jesus said at the outset of His public ministry. For thirty years, He cultivated a relationship with His Father that nobody knew about, that no one has any record of, that no one has written about extensively—or even at all, that I know of. But once His public ministry begins, it is evident where He has been: with God. That is why Nicodemus came and said, *"Rabbi, we know that you are a teacher who has come from God. For no one could perform the signs you are doing if God were not with him"* (John 3:2 NIV).

A *Pharisee* came to Him and said that, because he could see it. They knew! And they had a choice: they could either face the challenge to become better and to get right with God, or they could resist it and oppose it in a murderous way, which is what they did.

---

David was a man after God's own heart when he was completely unknown publicly. David worshipped God in spirit and in truth long before he established systems of worship during his forty-year reign as king in Jerusalem. It was the secret place that qualified David and gave him that highest of titles that can be given to a man: "A Man After God's Own Heart." That badge of honor came to David because he proved he desired relationship with Yahweh above all else. His focus was not to prove his identity or to improve his position. Whether working as a shepherd, commanding an army, or later, serving as king, David remained focused on pursuing God's heart. And although David made mistakes and sinned greatly, he established something that God blessed richly, especially during David's son's Solomon's reign. God honored David because of what He and David had developed through relationship in the secret place.

---

At the outset of His ministry, Jesus was not merely teaching. He was exposing the hidden motives, the hidden agendas, the traditions, and the power base of those who controlled the people wrongly for so long. He was not just coming in with teachings to make the people say, "Ah! We get it now," or, "We feel good about this!" He was coming to say, "This is the teaching I'm bringing to you, and by doing so, I am exposing what you've always known."

That is why His enemies wanted to kill Him. From the very outset of Jesus' ministry—actually from His very birth—there was a plan to destroy Him because He was exposing everything that was wrong to bring everything that was right from Heaven to this earth.

John said, *"Even now, the ax is laid to the root of the trees"* (Matthew 3:10 NKJV). He did not say, "the base of the tree." If you are going to cut a tree down—and I have cut many —you lay the ax or the cutting instrument at the base of the tree. But John says the ax is laid at the *root* of the tree. He was speaking of the Pharisees, the scribes, the elders and the teachers of the law—the political power base, the religious power base of Israel. And he was saying, "Right now, what is beneath the surface"—note: the root is *beneath* the surface—"is being cut down! It is being exposed. It is being dealt with."

And it is because for so long there was so much hidden beneath the surface that was wrong. John confronted that, and so did the Lord. John came to prepare the way for Jesus to come and take it a step further: to not just expose what was wrong, but to bring what is right. As was the case in Jesus' day, it is possible today to get by with a form of greatness that lacks the values of Yahweh and the essence of character through which He desires to establish His Kingdom. It is possible to fake it in order to make it—but I assure you, any success as such will be short lived. Unless Heaven backs us up, all invitations, introductions, and any fruit thereof will be ephemeral. Genuine substance: that is what Heaven is after in us. Just as John paved the way for Jesus to bring the revelation of the Kingdom by exposing the hypocrisy and counterfeit greatness of that day, we must be prepared from the hidden place to respond with integrity when invitations and introductions are laid before us. When the path is one cleared from God, and we remain pure and real before Him and people, we can be assured of consistent and sustainable victories in our endeavors.

# CHAPTER 7

# Protocol

WE HAVE CONSIDERED THE SIGNIFICANCE of invitations and introductions as well as the part they play in obtaining and properly maintaining access into people's lives—individuals, their families, their networks of influence, organizations they may own or lead, etc. Continued access also depends on appropriate decorum and respect for protocol.

I was recently on assignment in a highly secretive part of a nation's military and intelligence establishment. Once I entered the building, my phone was locked up in a safety box. From that point on, I could not go anywhere in the building without being escorted. Any digression from the rules which governed that facility would disqualify me from further influence in that place. Every door had an access code which my escort had to key in. It is like that with relationships and access to realms of influence in general.

Protocol is the code of conduct that governs social and professional behavior. There is good protocol and bad protocol, meaning that in every setting there is potential for the display of both proper and improper codes of conduct. God's children who wish to grow consistently in influence at tables and platforms must learn and exercise proper protocol.

When we are invited to someone's table or platform, several dynamics must generally be in play before we even arrive:

**1. Measure of trust.** Very few people in our lives can be trusted with everything about our lives. However, when it comes to invitations to specific events or functions, hosts want to ensure that invitees can be trusted to benefit them and not hurt them in the context of the project at hand. Can they be trusted to carry out the assignment in a way that adds value to them and their organizations, etc.?

**2. Favor.** An invitation denotes a degree of favor with the host. That means the door is open for our input, and ideally, that openness facilitates deeper relationship.

**3. Honor and respect.** On both sides of the equation, host and invitee, there must be genuine value given for the person and accomplishment of each individual.

**4. Hospitality and generosity.** No one wants to serve a cause whose leaders are stingy and inhospitable; likewise, no host desires guests who are greedy, entitled, and unappreciative. A balance must be struck wherein hosts and those who serve their causes are mutually satisfied with each other's contributions towards the task at hand. The best way to ensure such harmony is to communicate expectations thoroughly ahead of time. My church board has a letter we forward to any new platform hosts who request my services. The letter clearly states the expectations for how I am treated in regard to travel, accommodation and compensation for my involvement. I recommend everyone who itinerates has a letter like this.

The Bible says we should not invite ourselves, overstay our welcome, return too often, or be in any way dishonorable towards our hosts. Proverbs 25:17 strongly states the sentiment this way:

> *Don't wear out your welcome*
> *by staying too long at the home of your friends,*
> *or they may get fed up with always having you there*
> *and wish you hadn't come.* (TPT)

Recognizing appropriate limits on a relationship is crucial in honoring a host who has asked us to share their table or platform. The apostle Paul advises us to give *"respect to whom respect is owed, honor to whom honor is owed"* (Romans 13:7 ESV). He goes so far as to state: *"Outdo one another in showing honor"* (Romans 12:10 ESV).

I have learned that once we are invited to a platform—once we are given access to a platform belonging to someone else—we have to recognize, honor and follow the processes and protocols that have been set in place for that particular platform. The host has paid a price in order to establish it, and both the platform and the event taking place are governed by a specific set of protocols. For example, one of my hosts over the years has made it clear that he is a stickler for punctuality. Speakers must arrive at the venue thirty minutes before the event, and not one minute later. Another host at a mega-church asked for detailed notes on the subject I would speak on. Even though I never have notes when I speak, I wrote some out to satisfy his requirement. On stage, he pointed out a large clock in the back of the building. He said, "You will be up at 11:45 on the dot. You must be finished by 12:30. If you are not finished, someone will step up and take the microphone away from you."

I asked him if I could give an appeal for individuals who might want to commit their lives to Christ.

He said, "No. Salvation is for next week."

Not my style; not my style at all. However, my agreement or disagreement with the way a certain leader leads his/her organization is completely immaterial to my adherence to protocol. Once I commit to an assignment, I choose to respect whatever guidelines govern that particular establishment. I will not step onto any platform without first choosing to submit to the authority of the person who has invited me. This is not difficult for me at all—because of honor. I recognize that others have paid a price to obtain or establish the platform (or table) and I honor their vision, labor, and all the process they went through to develop things to that point.

Submitting to the authority of the platform host is of paramount importance. Otherwise, we ourselves cannot draw from the extensive power and authority that we have in Christ to minister on that platform. If we try to take over, we cannot operate effectively when we enter someone else's domain of influence and responsibility. On a personal note, I don't concern myself with any part of a conference that does not have to do with my specific assignment. My job is to speak and to grow in relationship with my hosts: period. I do not offer input on how things can be improved unless I am asked. I do not evaluate someone else's team or family, and I do not get involved with any matters pertaining to the internal operations of a platform, especially concerning finances or staff. I remain positive throughout the meetings, and if issues do need to be dealt with, I may address them, but usually not until long after the event is over. That gives me time to find the best approach.

While on assignment, Danielle and I were once hosted by a precious Armenian lady in Cyprus. The moment we entered her home, this wonderful and gracious host said, "My house is your house. Everything here is available to you." Although we knew our host was sincere in her offer, we also knew better than to treat every part of her house as our own. She did not have to tell us that there were parts of her house—her closets, drawers, safes—that we should not access. Yet she said, "It is all yours." Protocol teaches us not to go into places that we have no business being in.

Let's go a bit deeper by looking at the variables and dynamics often associated with platform and table assignments. When we are invited to various venues, whether to a church, a gathering of people with a common purpose and desire, a governmental agency, or a business entity, we must take into consideration *who* invited us. Then, we should consider what is the *purpose* of the invitation? What objective is this person or group trying to accomplish by having us on that platform? Once we have answered these questions, we can determine how to best carry out our task and meet the expectations of our hosts. By taking time to evaluate the specifics, and then being able to come in with the proper perspective and follow good protocol, we maximize the potential we can have through that platform.

Adherence to protocol means we must be able to recognize and adapt to the change from a platform to a table. There are differences in how those are governed—even if the same hosts handle both settings within a short period of time. I'll illustrate this dynamic with a personal experience.

Some time ago, I was invited to speak at an event put on by individuals well-networked with the government of their nation. On the day of the event, numerous members of that country's parliament and other governmental agencies were in the audience with their families and entourages, including security details. I'm certain that for so many governmental leaders to be present at the meeting, long-standing relationships had been tapped into and favors had been pulled. The leadership of the organization sponsoring the event had done all the footwork. The place buzzed with power and prestige.

After I spoke at the event, several opportunities arose for me to be at the table with legislators and other political figures who had listened to my talk. The leader of the organization putting on the event came to me and announced, "For lunch you are going to sit at my table with the following individuals…" and he named the offices the table guests held. Immediately, I became aware that we were shifting from platform to table. Indeed, we moved from the large auditorium where I had stood on a platform directly into a banquet hall in the same complex.

When you sense that the scene is shifting from platform to table, it is important to understand the difference in dynamics. Because the relational dynamics and protocols of a table are quite different from those of a platform, it is important to recognize the moment when you shift from table to platform, or from platform to table, so that you can flow with the workings thereof.

The primary focus of the table is relationship. At the table, we must focus on cultivating relationship while serving the purposes of our host. The host is usually the person who says, "This is what we are going to do. This is the meeting we are going to have. This is the restaurant where we are going to meet. These are the people who are going to be around the table."

> *The primary focus of the table*
> *is relationship.*

Whoever sets up the table meeting must be the person we choose to serve in that situation. We must not serve our own purposes. We must not serve our own initiatives. We must not serve our own interests. We serve the host's purposes and interests. We move to the table from a platform, or we start at a table to begin something that could end up on a platform, all for the purpose of building relationship and serving the needs or desires of our host.

While we certainly need to keep the host in mind, we also need to think about the individuals whom the host has invited. If they are dignitaries, as in the example I just related, we must consider their positions and bring the appropriate measure of respect and honor to the encounter. I recall whispering to my host on my way to the table, "What do I call them? How do I address them?" Above all, I want to make sure that I exhibit appropriate manners and responses at the table. I do not want to say something in the way I address these individuals that from the very outset of the conversation takes me out of their league, so to speak.

The governmental leaders at the event I discussed above had seen me on a platform, and they seemed to like what they saw and heard. Next, they wanted to meet me in person. They wanted me to sit at their table. Appropriate conduct at the table was important if I was to keep building off the credibility the platform had already afforded. It is imperative to understand the difference between relating to crowds while on the platform and relating with individuals face-to-face at a table.

When it comes to our conversation in a table setting, we need first and foremost to hold back on taking any initiative where we are not the host. Your initiative must go out the door when you enter a table situation by invitation, because the one who invited you needs to lead, even to the point where he or she is the one who tells you where to sit.[4] That person has in his or her mind exactly how they want this meeting to go. They want you sitting next to a particular person, whether it is their spouse, their brother, their friend or the dignitary that they bring to the table. That is the person they want you to cultivate relationship with. They get to set the table, and then with the motive of serving them and building relationship, you take the seat where you are told to sit.

In table conversations, my approach has always been to answer questions rather than initiate topics. If conversation becomes awkward and I am given a lot of opportunity to speak, I ask questions to generate conversation. The key with this is to

---

4 See Luke 14:8 and 10.

say very little about ourselves. They have already seen us on the platform. As a result of what they saw on the platform, they want to grow this brief acquaintance into some kind of relationship. Otherwise, the table meeting would not be happening. There is no need to promote ourselves at a table. There is no need to advertise our presence. We are there by invitation, by request.

With relationship at the forefront of honoring and serving my host, my approach has always been to remain quiet until I am asked to speak. I follow the flow of the conversation and the host's agenda. I listen to the conversations going on, never interjecting, and not offering my opinion. I am not saying everyone must do that. It is what I have done, and it has worked well for me. I maintain a back seat to the whole event until someone puts me in the front seat by asking me a question or requesting my opinion. If they want me to have a voice in what is being spoken about or if they want me to contribute to a topic by directing that conversation somewhere in particular, they are going to have to initiate that. I will not. As I've stated repeatedly, I prefer the concealed phase of hiddenness over that of being revealed. Even just minutes after being revealed to an audience on a platform, I will choose concealment at a table.

On the flip side, I have witnessed what happens when the guest of honor or other individuals invited to the table took it upon themselves to usurp the direction of a meeting away from the host—a disaster, socially and relationally. If the host is a quiet and reserved individual, a guest might presume to take over and steer the conversation to his or her own purposes. Big mistake! Nothing sets a host off more than that. I promise you, even the kindest, most discrete hosts are aware that *they* are hosting that meeting. They should be honored. Hosts must be given the respect they deserve to direct the conversation at the table in their own way. Guests cannot take over. I cannot emphasize that enough.

Once the direction of the conversation is initiated, we should try to respond with simple sentences, not elaborate explanations or complicated answers. It is important to demonstrate the character and wisdom of God in those situations and not move on tangents. Stay on point. Answer the questions. Focus on whoever asked the question, not simply on giving the answer.

*Platform and table meetings*
*represent opportunities to give, not take.*

Moreover, *what* we say in a table setting is important. If there are agendas within us to build ourselves in the estimation of others at the table, to strengthen our own interests or our own platform, these motives must be checked at the door before we enter a table situation. Otherwise, those personal motives will show up in our conversation. People of influence—those who are well-educated, who have paid a price to be in a position, individuals with authority of any kind in any field—can pick out a selfish motive from far away. They will pick it up within a few minutes. The more we talk, the more we reveal who we are. If there are motives in us that are not pure, they *will* manifest.

So at a table meeting I let the host—the person who is paying the bill and facilitating the whole thing—take the initiative to direct the conversation. Speaking of paying the bill —this is purely personal and does not have to be everyone's standard—there is rarely a scenario in which I sit at a table that I do not offer to pay the bill. My offer is genuine; I will be very happy to pay. Often, when I know my paying the bill will not offend my host, I will sneak away during the meal and pay.

My general attitude at every platform and table meeting is that I am there to give, not to take. I prepare for platform events by purchasing thoughtful and generous gifts for my hosts.

Sometimes that process begins months before I fly out to meet my hosts. I am not big on after-the-event thank you notes: I prefer to show gratitude and generosity on the front end of an assignment. It helps set the spiritual atmosphere for what I am there to accomplish. I also prepare to sow generously in venues where offerings are received and there are opportunities to give during presentations or teachings. Generally, I want to demonstrate that I place personal value on what I was invited to participate in, and I want my financial seed in that good soil.

One more personal practice: I always make myself available to roll up my sleeves and offer help with anything that needs to be done, be it setting up chairs, moving sound equipment, or even picking up trash. I am there to serve, and my service is not confined to holding a microphone and speaking to an audience. Many times, especially in new relationships, I am treated somewhat like a celebrity. People are assigned to carry things for me, and on several occasions I have even had bodyguards (not in dangerous places, mind you). Though I appreciate sentiments of honor and excellent service, I do not find celebrity-status treatment beneficial, especially within the body of Christ. Whenever the church world has lifted up individuals on Hollywood-like pedestals in the past, we have been disappointed in the long run. When I sense an environment of celebrity-status speakers, I immediately try to level the playing field by serving.

> *You are not only responsible for being on stage,*
> *but for setting it.*

I have been inspired by the story of a well-known movie star, who is noted for being the first on the set every morning whenever he is shooting a film. He makes himself available to every person involved, including camera operators, stagehands, and other crew members. When asked about this practice, he said that he values the opportunity to serve others and that his service helps win the respect of those involved with the project. That makes for a better filming environment in general. He says he sees himself as one who is not only responsible for *being* on stage, but also for *setting* it.

---

The importance of protocol cannot be overemphasized. Good protocol can be a game-changer in a positive sense; poor protocol can be a deal-breaker. It's all about the details.

When our boys were little, our family spent a couple of years following Nascar racing on television. Most races were on Sunday afternoons, so after church we would plant ourselves in front of the TV and watch the race. I vividly remember one race in which a race car costing between one hundred and two hundred thousand dollars was rendered completely useless on the track, because of a $0.35 part that malfunctioned right at the finish of the race. A tiny part cost a Nascar driver and team the entire race. If we liken the $100,000.00 car to someone operating on a platform or a table—say, a guest speaker—the $0.35 part is the generally invisible, yet critical adherence to protocol on and off the stage.

Good protocol is found in the details that go unnoticed by most, but are always noted by those who are responsible for the tables and platforms to which we are invited. Just like good nutrients benefit our bodies at the molecular and even atomic level, ultimately, good protocol helps us securely and consistently build relationships and influence.

# CHAPTER 6

# Vehicles of Influence

WHEN WE FOLLOW PROTOCOL, maintain pure motives, and carry ourselves with honor and integrity, tables and platforms become vehicles that can carry us, through relationship, deeper into people's hearts, families, organizations, even nations. But before we can begin to understand how a table or a platform can facilitate greater impact, we must understand what having influence looks like from Heaven's perspective.

The rhetoric used in many sermons and exhortations we hear in the church world is often very dynamic. The gospel of the Kingdom continually affirms and inspires us. It motivates us to win souls, do mighty works, and take ground for God—to be the agents of transformation in the earth. Those of us within the church applaud and celebrate messages conveying our authority and influence in this world. And yet, the true impact of any and all church presentations is not measured by what happens *within* the church itself, i.e., among the members of any particular congregation, ministry group, or the broader body of Christ worldwide. Impact can only be gauged by fruit—specifically, the kind that remains. Genuine transformation is that variety of fruit.

We can ask: after hearing thousands upon thousands of sermons, is the church body truly having an impact in this world? I do not mean by way of "decisions made for Christ," but by evidence of lives radically transformed. Are we genuinely influential as evidenced by having doors opened to the realms of legislation and government? Are we sought after as consultants to the leading influencers of our day? Is the church a catalyst for change—the kind that aligns the world more with its Creator's heart? Or is our credibility confined to church audiences and the church's organizational structure?

It is my conviction that Christians have over-focused on the gospel of salvation—including healing, signs, and miracles—at the expense of engaging with, growing in, and manifesting the gospel of the Kingdom. Winning souls is wise and important, but not more important than the broader gospel salvation belongs to which is the way of life Jesus demonstrated. That way of life affects lives and effects transformation on every level. Preaching to churched souls about winning lost souls confines us to church life, and that was never Jesus' plan when He established the church.

*Ekklesia*—the word our Lord used when announcing the church's inception and setting Peter as chief spokesperson for it —was not a word Jesus invented. He was using a word well-understood in the culture of that day. *Ekklesia* was the chief governing body in the ancient Greek world. The ekklesia dealt with legislation and governance. Its focus was outward, not inward. When the Lord said, *"Upon this rock I will build my church"* (Matthew 16:18 KJV), He was declaring into existence the body that would govern on His behalf: a body that, as the ekklesia, would influence every facet of society. We have erroneously reduced the ekklesia to meetings and church programs, endless treatises on doctrine, and well-meaning, yet misaligned attempts to "win souls."

A brief description of the early church in Acts 2 offers remarkable insight into the dynamics that enabled that church

—and ours if we follow its pattern—to be credible and influential.

> *And they continued steadfastly in the apostles' doctrine and fellowship, in the breaking of bread, and in prayers. Then fear came upon every soul, and many wonders and signs were done through the apostles. Now all who believed were together, and had all things in common, and sold their possessions and goods, and divided them among all, as anyone had need.*
>
> *So continuing daily with one accord in the temple, and breaking bread from house to house, they ate their food with gladness and simplicity of heart, praising God and having favor with all the people. And the Lord added to the church daily those who were being saved.* (Acts 2:42–47 **NKJV**)

One day I read this passage and the following sentence was highlighted to me as if it was lit up on the page: *"So continuing daily with one accord in the temple...." Continuing* somewhere (in the temple in this case) implies that whatever was being continued had begun somewhere else. In other words, the state of being in one accord did not start at the temple, it only continued there. Where did it begin? The next part of the sentence tells us: they were *"...breaking bread from house to house...."*

What has always been hailed as the early church's success (its explosive growth and powerful impact) did not emanate so much from daily corporate gatherings in the temple but rather from the smaller meetings that were held in people's homes. In fact, we know nothing about what took place in the temple, but various portions in the Book of Acts shed light on what believers did when they met in houses.

We don't know much about the large groups of disciples who followed Jesus, but we do know about the twelve—those mentioned by name as a group whom Jesus chose to work with closely:

*And He went up on the mountain and called to Him those He Himself wanted. And they came to Him. Then He appointed twelve, that they might be with Him and that He might send them out to preach, and to have power to heal sicknesses and to cast out demons.* (Mark 3:13–15 NKJV)

When the twelve came onto the platform of Jesus, they had to recognize that if they were to be part of it, they needed to operate under the terms He set for its establishment. But because of what they had seen demonstrated in their culture, the disciples had a faulty perception of greatness. They saw greatness as exemplified by the Pharisees, the scribes, the elders and the teachers of the law, who often lorded their positions over others. The markers of greatness in that culture included such things as being given the best seats in gatherings, having exalted titles, wearing fine clothes, possessing the nicest things and so forth (all with the wrong motives). To the disciples' way of thinking, these were the attributes and the evidence of greatness. They wanted to be seen as great. We know this as they argued about who would be the greatest.

*… [Jesus] came to Capernaum. And when He was in the house He asked them, "What was it you disputed among yourselves on the road?" But they kept silent, for on the road they had disputed among themselves who would be the greatest.* (Mark 9:33–34 NKJV)

Is it any wonder they sought a platform that resembled the "greatness" they had observed in their culture? That was likely what they thought they would personally experience by being on the platform of Jesus.

The broader public in Jesus' time was no better. They had a completely different perspective of how this Jesus-phenomenon should be handled. In their view, it was okay for Him to bring a message of freedom, a message of deliverance followed by signs, wonders and great miracles. They were thinking, "This must be our time as the nation of Israel to overthrow the yoke of oppression from the Roman government, to be independent and free from their rule." So, they wanted to utilize the platform of Jesus to make Him king and accomplish their own dreams of national independence. We read about the people who tried to do just that: *"Therefore when Jesus perceived that they were about to come and take Him by force to make Him king, He departed again to the mountain by Himself alone"* (John 6:15 NKJV). The people wanted to make Him king. But Jesus withdrew from them because He recognized that being an earthly king was not the purpose for which He had come. Yet Israel had been conditioned since the days of Saul becoming king through Samuel's anointing to always have a king over them, so that was the lens through which the public perceived Jesus in His humanity.

> The platforms of the Kingdom
> are to serve the purposes of Heaven
> rather than ambition, aspiration or selfish desire.

Jesus had to establish for His disciples as well as for the broader public that their perceptions of greatness and what they thought the outworking of His destiny should look like were not the terms on which His platform was built. His platform was not built to establish earthly rule over people in a nation or a region. His platform was not for the establishment of a natural government. Even now, the platform of Jesus has a much greater purpose—a heavenly purpose—with spiritual ramifications that will change the world forever.

Jesus Himself set the terms for how His platform was to operate. He came to demonstrate, manifest and lead us into a greater way. His way can be stated like this: the greater the platform, the more you serve. As in the case of the movie star's example, stated in the previous chapter, the greater the platform, the more we must humble ourselves—not exalt ourselves. This is especially true for believers because the platforms of the Kingdom are to serve the purposes of Heaven rather than our own individual ambitions, aspirations or selfish desires.

When I return from a trip where I was given much honor through tables and platforms alike, I follow a specific pattern of re-entry into my family and church life. One of my self-assigned tasks is that of serving my children and wife in the house, and also my co-laborers at the church. I find things I can do for them—even small things—whereby I intentionally disconnect from the honor that had been given to me during my assignment. Serving others protects me from pride that would try to set in, and it enables me to recalibrate my heart to the responsibility of being a husband, father, and leader. The ability to seamlessly transition from a platform experience to what might seem the mundane details of daily life comes from a heart sincerely dedicated to serving wherever the Father has us, not just when we are seen and recognized in a big arena during a revealed phase, but also in the small, unseen, concealed phase. Once again, it's all about the perspective we gain in living from the hidden place.

> *The greater the platform,*
> *the more you serve.*

In creation, everything we perceive to be spectacularly large has an even more infinite and astonishing complexity at its smallest level. For example, a magnificent mountain that stands over 15,000 feet tall can be taken down to the molecular, atomic, and even the nano (sub-atomic) level. It is the small that constitutes the big, not the other way around. The appearance of the large mountain is ultimately the exponential product of the sum of billions and billions of atoms, which are their own individual signs and wonders in their makeup and operations.

The success of the early church hinged on its community-building through small gatherings, not corporate meetings. The same pattern is seen in the way the Lord trained his disciples. In both cases, what developed by way of substance and character on a small scale eventually manifested as something world-changing. The better we build the small, the more secure the big can become. If we build something right, it can also become big. When we build big with the wrong mindset or structure, what we build can lack the essence that will ensure long-lasting fruitfulness. We must build small while thinking big—then the small is in the right environment for growth and development. I like to say it this way: *Big* must have a well-built *small* within it in order to remain big and grow.

---

We need to pay attention when scriptures reveal examples of individuals who get their way with kings and rulers. For example, Paul asked the governor, Festus, for audience with King Agrippa—and it was granted. Likewise, when he stood before Agrippa he sought audience with the Roman Emperor in Rome, and King Agrippa consented as well. Another person who seems to have had the right touch with rulers was Joseph of Arimathea. Interestingly, while very few things are mentioned about him, they are found in all four Gospels. Joseph of Arimathea is not a hero like the prophet Daniel or King David, but he steps in at a critical moment and accomplishes something significant. Joseph of Arimathea was the man who asked Pontius Pilate for the body of Jesus so he could bury the Lord in his own tomb. He asked for what is arguably the most controversial body in history, on Pilate's worst day, and it was granted to him. Like the house-to-house activities of the early church, God's people in the examples above exerted influence on a small scale, one-to-one. Their stories illustrate the big results which can come from relatively hidden meetings—table meetings—rather than from platforms.

The greatest influencers do not flaunt their power and authority, nor do they leverage it for insignificant concessions. They wait for moments when, as in the case of Joseph of Arimathea and Pilate, the stakes are high. Then they make their move. Joseph was undoubtedly a hidden one in the concealed phase of hiddenness. The Bible says he was *"a disciple, but secretly…"* (John 19:38 NKJV). He was wealthy and influential but kept a low profile until it was time to be revealed. Joseph's influence was never on a platform; it was at a table. He was known at tables and he did all his groundwork for influence there. Joseph was comfortable in and knew his place—both with what he had (table influence) and with what he did not have (a platform).

Someone asked me recently, while making small talk: "What types of people are most impressive to you these days?" I responded: "Those who know their place and remain grateful for what they are and what they are not, simultaneously."

---

Establishing credibility with people and being able to have influence among them is not a destination; it is a journey. We begin somewhere and we continually move deeper into hearts, lives, and ultimately organizations—even governments and nations. Tables and platforms have the capacity to be reliable, effective and powerful vehicles on such journeys. And they can be all-terrain vehicles at that, meaning there is no limit to where they can take us.

When Danielle and I started out in ministry, we had no idea —none whatsoever—what God would make available to us over time. Our worldview pertaining to influence was confined to the church world. At that point to us, an influential leader was one who filled a church with people and preached anointed sermons. We didn't know who we truly were or what was possible through our relationship with God and each other. Even so, we did our best to steward every table and every platform opportunity.

> *Being faithful with the small things*
> *establishes our identity and character,*
> *and allows us to gain influence at tables or platforms*
> *as invitations arise.*

In my early days of public ministry, I remember being involved with wedding ceremonies. My job was simply to say one prayer at the beginning or at the end, while my senior pastor conducted the rest of the service. I often laid awake preparing my heart for that one prayer. I wanted to speak well and have grace and power on my words. I remember standing at gravesites in the rain, committing the deceased to the grave and speaking words of comfort to family members who remained. To be honest, these were not my favorite assignments, but I put my all into them just the same. After rigorous international travel and great personal expense, Danielle and I spoke in meetings where only a handful of people turned up. We began serving at our current church leadership assignment with only about twenty parishioners. We have treasured every moment; we wouldn't want it any other way. From our perspective at the time, our response was about being faithful with the small things. From Heaven's point of view, our identity and character were being established, and we were being transported through tables and platforms deeper into the realms of our Father's Kingdom.

Anything is possible for you if you believe and persevere. Everything is available to you—in Him! Stay the course.

Celebrate the small assignments and give them your all. Steward every relationship and every opportunity. Your potential influence begins (and can end) in the metamorphosis of relationships you are invited into, from the most intimate of tables to the most expansive stage of an international platform. Whether you find yourself concealed or revealed, operate from the hidden place with integrity. Most of all, enjoy the journey, no matter the vehicle.

# CHAPTER 7

# Hosts and Guests

FOR THE PURPOSES OF OUR DISCUSSION, I present *hosts* as the individuals or groups that facilitate platform events and table meetings. *Guests* are the individuals with whom hosts co-labor to fulfill the objectives of such gatherings. Through years of itinerant speaking engagements within a certain movement or stream, and due to the fact that I associate with people who insist on speaking engagements that are founded on solid, long-lasting relationships, I have often found myself being a platform guest for some friends one week, and a host of a conference (involving both tables and platforms) with the same friends a few days or weeks later.

As I reflect on and draw from more than a decade of platform and table experience, I present here some of the inner workings of hosting and "guest-ing," particularly in the area of taking responsibility before, during, and after events.

I cannot emphasize enough the importance of the preparation of heart and spirit on both the host's and guest's part, long before a table gathering is planned or a platform event is scheduled to take place. Thirty years after my military service, the words of one of my captains still ring in my ears: "You never prepare for battle *during* the battle; you prepare beforehand." The host's chief responsibility is to prepare everything possible logistically and spiritually, both in terms of practical arrangements as well as in prayer and engagement with God's heart. Doing so facilitates an environment in which everyone involved can contribute and receive optimally. The guest's most important job in preparation is to fully understand the host's objective for the gathering or event.

Every platform event and every table meeting has a purpose. The host who orchestrates the occasion and has responsibility for what takes place also sets the course and purpose, whether the gathering is held in a stadium, a conference room, on a back-yard patio, in a kitchen, living room or restaurant. Wise guests invited to participate in a meeting will discern or discover the purpose ahead of time, and they will position and carry themselves accordingly. Certainly, one may ask the host the purpose of the event directly, but often a gathering has both an outward and an underlying purpose, and the host may not necessarily disclose the latter in advance.

A few years ago, a friend who owns and runs several businesses heard me speak at a platform event, which was a business breakfast. He later invited me to a table meeting to be held at a renowned seafood restaurant. He said, "Listen, I'd love for you to come out tonight. One of my business partners will be joining us."

I thanked my friend for the invitation and asked for the time and place, as well as other pertinent details.

Before giving me the specifics I requested, my friend continued, "This particular business is a significant new venture for us. I've been working on it with my partner for quite some time now. He's bringing his wife and children. I would love for you to meet them."

The dinner gathering had been presented to me as an opportunity to have a good time among friends and to facilitate the introduction between my friend's partner and me. However, because my friend emphasized how important the new business was and that he wanted me to meet the partner's family, I began to engage with a potential unspoken agenda.

I engaged with the Lord that afternoon to see if I could get a hold of the blueprint for that evening's meeting. During my time of prayer, it became clear to me that my friend wanted me to evaluate his partner. In order to gauge whether I thought he could trust that man for some big things they were about to undertake together in business, my friend wanted to see my response to his partner in the course of our conversation at the table. My friend never spoke to me about that agenda beforehand.

This example shows the importance of engaging with the purpose of a table meeting in the spiritual dimension in advance, especially when we have time beforehand. Regarding this particular case, I made the right call. Not only were insightful things shared in the meeting where I was able to release the wisdom of God into some aspects of my friend's new business, but when the meeting was over, as I was hugging my friend goodnight, I whispered in his ear concerning his partner: "You can trust him. I believe he's one of us."

> *Engaging with the purpose of a meeting ahead of time can allow you to create a mirror image of Heaven on earth concerning that assignment.*

My whispered comment was insightful and encouraging for my friend; it was a response which pleased him immensely. He wrote me a note a few days later: "I really appreciated your posture in the whole meeting, but especially what you said at the end. I really needed to hear that."

The meeting had an underlying purpose which I needed to know in advance. If I had not taken the time to engage with

Yahweh and had not seen the hidden purpose and spoken into it, as far as my friend the host goes, his purpose for that table meeting would have fallen short. I had to be able to discern and speak to his agenda. And as for me, out of that table meeting came more platform and more table opportunities in the years ahead.

---

Let us take a look at the host's side of things in terms of preparation. As a host and facilitator for tables and platforms, a profound weight of responsibility settles on me as I sit on my mountain (my place of authority for that particular undertaking) to engage with the task at hand. In terms of platform events, when I invite someone—whether to co-labor in writing a book, participate in an online interview, or as guest speaker in our church—my preoccupation is with giving my guest proper honor. The logistics of the event usually lie with the amazing team of leaders and volunteers who work alongside me. They are remarkable at what they do, and I give them highest honor for their part. The role of giving honor to my guest, however, rests on me as host.

I prepare for the personalized moments we will share together. I prepare in prayer and engage with the assignment by going into the heavenly realms and looking at that assignment. From that perspective, I can see what is already established. Then I am able to administrate and govern properly here in this realm, so that what happens here mirrors what God already has in His heart. Whether we are host or guest, engaging with the purpose of a meeting ahead of time can enable us to create a mirror image of Heaven on earth concerning that assignment. As we do, Heaven is attracted to whatever looks like itself and can manifest itself on or through that earthly reflection.

That's why Solomon built the temple to the particular specifications he received from Heaven: what he built on earth was as it was in Heaven. When you structure something according to Heaven's plan, whether it be a physical building or a spiritual platform, the glory comes, settles over what is built on earth, and does not depart from there. Then, that glory can go from that platform into every segment and aspect of society. In Solomon's time, Israel became the nation whose platform everybody wanted to trade into and receive from. Israel's platform became the place that all the surrounding nations paid tribute to because they recognized that partnership with Israel's platform benefitted their own platforms.

Our source for the authority to establish a platform must be the Father, the Son and the Holy Spirit. When this, the most harmonious relationship existing in Heaven, co-labors with us on earth, it breathes into and through us, releasing a Kingdom measure of influence through whatever platform we are instructed to build.

It all goes back to relationship, and focusing on relationship brings us right back to tables. I am more fascinated with tables than I am with platforms. I prefer a table over a platform any day. I am not impressed with large numbers. People always ask me how many people were in attendance at this or that meeting. The truth is, sometimes in platform assignments I speak to large crowds and sometimes to small crowds.

But I treasure table opportunities the most. The key to tables is relationship. While platforms are connected to relationship, tables are about intimate conversation, up close and personal. At the table, your personal issues become visible and known to those with you, and their issues become known to you. You come together, sometimes working through differences. As I have said many times, in many contexts, relationship is of paramount importance, especially in the Kingdom.

I have observed that the church has focused much more on building a platform for ministry than on developing one-on-one relationships. That was my own experience for many years. Reflecting the conditioning that we have been raised in, those of us who are ministers have focused on getting a platform and on trying to make a name for ourselves. There are not necessarily bad motives behind that focus. We may want to build a platform in order to establish a message or a movement to impact the broader population for the Kingdom, whether it be in our city, in our nation or in the world as a whole. But I have found that even such a noble purpose is better served if first we cultivate personal relationships that are solid, relationships that are outstanding, relationships that are upright and wholesome—relationships that are pure.

> *Whether you serve as host or guest,*
>
> *honor is key.*

Competitiveness must never be found among us. Rather we must be marked by the honoring of one another, learning, and improving. Danielle and I honor our friends with whom we often minister on platforms around the world, namely, Ian Clayton, Grant and Sam Mahoney, Lindi Masters, and Stephen Mckie. Whenever one of us is up to speak, the others form a cheering section, from which they continually express agreement with what is being said and support for the person speaking. We celebrate each other's differences, and we value the unique piece every person contributes to the whole. It is a pure joy to co-labor with these men and women.

---

Whether you find yourself in the position of host or guest, honor is key. If you are a guest, remember you have been invited to participate at someone else's table or on their platform. To respect the work they have done to establish it, allow them to guide the discussion at the table, and follow the protocols they have set for the platform. By doing so, you honor them. If you are a host, ensure the logistics of the table or platform are covered well, and prepare for your guest through sincere, prayerful engagement over the meeting. If you honor them, you honor God and advance His Kingdom in the earth.

# CHAPTER 8

# Friends of Kings

IN 1 KINGS 4 WE FIND A LIST OF PEOPLE who served as King Solomon's officials. One of them was *"Zabud the son of Nathan, a priest and the king's friend"* (1 Kings 4:5 NKJV). I have been inspired by this verse for years. I imagine much could have been written about Zabud, as he undoubtedly had a full and fascinating life. And yet, he is presented to us in scripture simply as the king's friend. Zabud's task was to *be* someone for the king, not just to *do* things for him. I have studied the Bible and I have sought Yahweh over the years for insight regarding the qualities of a king's friend. How can we attain the kind of influence that renders us as valuable to rulers of our day as Zabud was to Solomon?

The Book of Proverbs gives us a clue: *"He that loves pureness of heart and has grace on his lips, the king shall be his friend"* (22:11 KJ2000).

When we study individuals in scripture who not only stood before kings, but impacted kings' lives (Esther, Mordecai, Daniel, Joseph, the apostle Paul, and prophets such as Nehemiah, Isaiah, Jeremiah), we find that every one of them possessed the two key qualities listed in Proverbs 22:11—purity of heart and grace on their lips. In my book, *Weaponized Honor*, I examined the relationship of individuals like Daniel and Joseph to the various rulers they served, and I pointed out that because of purity of heart and grace on their lips, kings valued them highly.

When Esther stood before the king, and later when Mordecai ruled from the place that Haman had ruled from before; when Joseph took the reins over Egypt to save the nations from starvation; when Nehemiah spoke to the king and requested resources to rebuild the walls of the city of God, of Jerusalem, they operated out of the kingly capacity Yahweh had given them. That capacity was perhaps rooted in what they had obtained during their own seasons of hiddenness and prayer. And when in their governance, the authority for dominion—in Greek, the *exousia*—came to them from their time in the secret place, these heroes of our faith carried power and authority when they stood before kings. Rulers recognized the radiance and glory from another realm. These individuals were awakened to their identity as heirs of God: consequently, they had confidence when they stood before kings. Their awareness of their position as sons of God (or, sons and daughters—the use of *sons* in the Scriptures often denotes both genders) allowed them to bring the kingdoms of the world into alignment with the Kingdom of our Lord and of His Christ and to reign with Him on the earth.

---

The *pureness of heart* mentioned in Proverbs 22:11 is a remarkable quality. I believe we become what we set our hearts on. If we love pureness of heart, we will engage with pureness of heart. We will desire that purity; we will value it. We will guard our hearts from anything that makes them impure. The purity of our hearts reflects the quality of our character and the integrity in our intentions. Purity enables us to honor protocol, as presented above. Purity establishes the code inside of us that determines our behavior, our thought processes, and the way our spirit, soul, and body operate, not just in front of kings, but in front of everyone. I believe that is why we speak of someone as being pure (or not being pure, for that matter) rather than saying "He/she has purity." In other words, purity is not something we put on; it is a state of being.

Kings (not just those in the formal position of king, but influencers of economies, society, culture, etc.), by virtue of their calling and assignment, have an extraordinary capacity to discern right from wrong. Proverbs 20:8 says, *"A king who sits on the throne of judgment scatters all evil with his eyes"* (NKJV). Kings, especially those who are wholesome and upright in their ways, have the ability to know if someone or something is off. Amazingly, in my experience, even unrighteous rulers possess discernment about good and evil, in spite of their own wrongdoings. Thus, we can deduce that kings have an enhanced sense for purity. They know when those who come before them have pure or impure motives, if they have hidden agendas or offer genuine relationship, even friendship. The images we form from storybook kingdoms of kings feasting at banqueting tables, holding scepters, sitting on thrones and making decrees give us a romantically unrealistic picture of what it means to embody true royal authority. Kings are to leverage their position, to lay their lives down, to utilize everything they have to help those for whom they are responsible. And whoever those kings are, if we are invited to be before them, we are to come with pure hearts.

A pure heart houses integrity. It has no agenda to get something from the king. In the context of our modern world, a pure heart does not desire to name drop, brag about a relationship with an influential person on social media, or to wear it as a badge of honor and notoriety. True friends of kings walk with integrity, value confidentiality, and have no desire for anything the king has except the honor and privilege they have to be in relationship. Such proper conduct and protocol stems from a pure heart.

Beyond pureness of heart, the other half of the description from the friends-of-kings verse—of *grace on his lips*—is equally significant. This is especially true when we are in relationship with someone of influence who does not share our belief system or standards. To have grace on our lips means we interact with someone from a place of truly valuing that person, their position, the Heaven-ascribed value in the individual, without expectations of adherence to our own ethical, moral or operational standards. We perceive the king as a friend entrusted to our love and care by God, and thus, we do not accuse or judge them in our hearts.

> *Proper conduct and protocol*
> *stem from a pure heart.*

*Grace on our lips* is having no agenda of promoting or exalting ourselves over the weaknesses that we see in them. Every king makes mistakes, sometimes major ones. Those who govern and rule have a position of power, influence, and authority. They have many things to tend to, many people surrounding them, many agendas floating all over. And they are human: they have flaws that they are still working on, issues in their hearts that they need counsel to break through. They need input from Heaven. I believe those of us who truly get a hold of this concept—who as sons of God come before kings *as* kings—will be given the opportunity to see those flaws and be able to help people of influence to change. The key here in what the word of God instructs us is grace. We must have grace on our lips.

---

I recently met with a friend whom I consider a king, due to his enormous success in his field of endeavor. He is brilliant, industrious, influential, wealthy, and well-established in godly character and virtue. Though powerful and prominent, my friend has always been down-to-earth and sincere. He has a pure desire to interact, have fellowship, and share life with me. During our last meeting, within just minutes of our time together, it became clear to me that my friend had fallen into error and had engaged with something that would not enable him to maximize his potential.

Due to his involvement in high places and with people of great power, my friend had become entangled in reports regarding the evil that was taking place in the world by way of corruption, conspiracies and other vices. He had become fixated on observing evil instead of focusing on doing good. He was fascinated with stories through which dark deeds were exposed and confronted. Thus, he had lost his equilibrium in terms of dreaming about, building and carrying out his assignment. The Bible says, *"Do not be overcome by evil but overcome evil with good"* (Romans 12:21 NIV). My friend had done the opposite.

I listened to my friend and remained quiet until he shared all that was on his heart. And while hearing him out, I made a choice—the same choice that I make every time I face similar circumstances. It is something I have had to train myself in and develop. The choice is that I must put on grace and let everything I say and do stem from grace. If I was to have any chance to change the situation and to bring breakthrough to my friend, I would have to evaluate everything he said through the filter of grace. I had to choose to respond with grace on my lips, not condemnation.

When I was given a chance to respond, I was able to release God's word that was burning on my heart. I said to him, "Brother, there is a place for you in Heaven. I have to bring you up there with me right now. I have to show you how highly esteemed you are among our brothers and sisters there, before the elders, before the chancellors, before the Seven Spirits of

God, the men in white linen, the cloud of witnesses, and above all, before the Father, Son, and Holy Spirit."

The issue was not grotesque sin or anything of that nature. It was simply a focus in the wrong direction, which was "the other side." I continued, "Why spend energy focusing on that which is wrong or even vile in the practices in the agencies and industry you are involved with? Turn your gaze back to Heaven. Devote your time and energy to God's goodness and love. Engage with Yeshua, with what surrounds Him and with His throne. Become aware of the angels that hearken to the voice of His word. Your focus should be on everything that Heaven has for you."

He remained quiet, his eyes fixed on me.

I continued. "Listen, let us look into Heaven. Let me show you what you can embrace."

Within twenty minutes a powerful anointing came over me. I have been in many different settings while ministering, and there was a stronger anointing upon my life in that moment to speak to this king with grace than I had in all previous meetings combined. By the time I was done, he was *un*done.

Grace was the catalyst for his breakthrough. Grace—from my lips—was beckoning him: "Come up here. Look with me at the goodness of our Father. You have amazing potential. You are amazing. You have extraordinary creativity. You are gifted. You are blessed and all of Heaven rejoices and celebrates you. Stay in that realm. Stay in that place that you came from."

The outcome was exceptional. He was not stuck anymore. The place we were in was filled with the glory of the Lord, with the radiance of Yeshua. Everything shifted. Everything changed. I was able to see the transformation even in his outlook. There was a glow on the man after I was done.

The incident with this ruler raises another point that I must make. Correction of and instruction to leaders is to come at a table from those they have relationship with, not from a platform. I have no respect for leaders who get up and publicly blast other leaders. If any correction is to come, it should come at a table. If we do not have the relationship to correct someone at a table, then we must remain silent from the platform. We need to choose to leave them alone. We are not fixing anything or improving matters by maligning somebody else's name through the internet or any platform where we have influence.

––––––––––

Another factor in being able to be good friends to kings is to operate from the right mindset about who we are. When we obtain influence with the influential, and when we have opportunity to impact their lives, it is important that we do not appear before them with a "less-than" mindset. We must not interact with kings out of a place of need for attention or to seek handouts. Handouts may enable us to survive, but they will never lead us to financial significance with which we can really make a difference in the world. We must also not be infatuated with the position, wealth or prestige of individuals, whether they run corporations, nations or empires of wealth.

> *We are Christ's kings and priests.*
> *Therefore, we appear before kings as kings.*

We must come as sons who recognize we are in a meeting that Heaven has orchestrated. Though we must honor someone's position and status accordingly, in our hearts we always remember that we are Christ's kings and priests. Therefore, we appear before kings *as* kings.

Such was my stance some time ago, when I sat on a plane next to a prominent businessman. The interaction started awkwardly because the man was agitated, muttering under his breath as he took his seat beside me. "I always fly business class, but all the seats were taken. Now I have to sit here…"

"Next to me," I interjected.

He nodded, still flustered.

"No problem, sir," I said. "No offense taken. I would have been upset, too, if I had to sit next to *me* instead of in business class."

He laughed. The ice broke. Things improved from there.

About an hour into the flight, and after a few drinks, the man started to share about his life. He had been successful as a lawyer in New York. Consequently, he was wealthy. He told me he owned three homes in expensive areas in the U.S., and a summer home in a coastal suburb of Athens, Greece. I remained quiet during his monologue on his professional achievements and socio-economic status. I entered the state of hiddenness, and I trusted Yahweh for wisdom in how to conduct myself.

After dinner was served, the man turned to me and said he would appreciate my input on a dilemma he was facing. He said, "You seem like a smart guy." (Remember, I had barely spoken.) "I do not know which house to live in." He went on to describe the houses and the areas where they were located. "I am torn. Which house should I move to permanently? This is the big issue in my life right now."

I pondered his question for some time. Then I said, "Your dilemma does not have to do with the house itself or the area; rather, it is about the relationships with those who live in or near those houses. Your issue is a family matter."

The man lit up and loudly said, "You are way too young to have come up with a wise answer like that."

Our conversation continued throughout the flight. He had more questions, and I was able to offer much input into his life. By the time we landed, the man wanted to stay in touch, and he offered to make a contribution into my wife's humanitarian organization. He had come to find out about it by asking me questions such as, "Who are you? What world do you come from?"

Years ago, a man with the stature and assertiveness of this gentleman would have intimidated me into silence. But, having spent much time in the realms of my Father, I knew from the start that by divine appointment I was sitting next to a king, *as a king*. Surely, the businessman had attained something great and he was someone notable. But so am I, and so are you.

By God's grace we have been made whole in Christ, and we were given seats beside Him in heavenly places. What we carry is of utmost importance and valuable for our generation and for the generations yet to come. We must do everything possible to cultivate the right identity and mindset—we must know who we are before our Father, and we must cultivate the character within that will facilitate the fullness of the blessing of the Gospel through our lives.

# Epilogue

I BEGAN THIS BOOK BY SHARING MY EXPERIENCE with a young businessman. We met at a table, had a wonderful time together, and then he quickly attempted to take the heavenly substance we had partaken of at our table to a mega-church platform. I left the story at the point where I kindly turned down his offer and suggested we grow in relationship. Sadly, but not surprisingly, I never again heard from him. I am not surprised because I have come to understand how platform-oriented individuals, especially leaders, operate. Platform-builders often evaluate almost everything—their interactions with other people, the beauty of nature, inspirational moments found in literature, the arts, entertainment, or the lessons of life in general—with the thought, "Can this help build the platform?"

I believe the young man did not contact me again because my desire to go deeper at a table was a disruption to the norm in his life of always thinking, "Build the platform." It was as though I had pulled the cables of his electric circuit apart: "We met you; we like you; we think we can build our platform with you; will you come to us?" Somewhere between "we like you" and the invitation, I veered off the path he expected to the path I value most—that of relationship, of sharing life and walking together without a specific agenda in mind, of sitting together at the table. I treasure the table. I trust that in the pages of this book you received motivation to walk down the same path with me. It is on that path we find friendship, and that is where we have the opportunity to love deeply.

Remember, if we make the most of our tables, our platforms will flourish as well. More will be accomplished on platforms, and more fruit that remains will continually grow on the platform level, if we steward the tables well.

I'm certain you and I will interact somehow on the platform level again through another book, an upcoming conference, a webinar, TV show—who knows? But I also hope our Father will leverage the impact of this message to bring us together at a table as well. Until then, let us remain in His love, and let us continue to build what He is building on the earth and in the cosmos.

# About the Author

Marios Ellinas is an international speaker, author and consultant. He has numerous inspirational books and two spy thrillers. Marios lives in Connecticut, USA, with his wife and three children.

# OTHER BOOKS BY MARIOS ELLINAS

### Son of Thunder Publications

Weaponized Honor: Tactical Love, 2017

### Marios Ellinas Publications
### Non Fiction:

Sexy Laundry, 2018

Dirty Laundry, 2017
with Danielle Ellinas

High Level Clearance, 2013
with Patrick Lynch

Government Collision, 2012

The Next Test, 2011

Warrior Material, 2010

Running to the Impossible, 2008

### Fiction:

(Under pen name Trace Evans)
The Cargo, 2016
The Trade, 2015

## ...AND COMING IN 2020...
## *RULING CITIES*

*Find them all on Amazon.com*

Made in the USA
Columbia, SC
22 September 2019